CANAL WALKS—V

CHESHIRE AND STAFFORDSHIRE

BY

JOHN N. MERRILL

MAPS AND PHOTOGRAPHS

BY JOHN N. MERRILL

a J.N.M. PUBLICATION

1989

**JNM PUBLICATIONS,
WINSTER,
MATLOCK,
DERBYSHIRE.
DE4 2DQ**

Conceived, edited, typeset, designed, marketed and distributed by John N. Merrill.

First Published — July 1987

This edition — June 1989

ISBN 0 907496 38 2

Meticulous research has been undertaken to ensure that this publication is highly accurate at the time of going to press. The publishers, however, cannot be held responsible for alterations, errors or omissions, but they would welcome notification of such for future editions.

Printed by:

Set in Plantin — Roman and Bold.

Cover photograph: Macclesfield Marina, Canal and former Hovis Mill by John N. Merrill. © JNM Publications.

ABOUT THE WALKS -

Whilst every care is taken detailing and describing the walks in this book, it should be borne in mind that the countryside changes by the seasons and the work of man. I have described the walks to the best of my ability, detailing what I have found on the walk in the way of stiles and signs. Obviously with the passage of time stiles become broken or replaced by a ladder stile or even a small gate. Signs too have a habit of being broken or pushed over. All the routes follow rights of way and only on rare occasions will you have to overcome obstacles in its path, such as a barbed wire fence or electric fence.

The seasons bring occasional problems whilst out walking which should also be borne in mind. In the height of summer paths become overgrown and you will have to fight your way through in a few places. In low lying areas the fields are often full of crops, and although the pathline goes straight across it may be more practical to walk round the field edge to get to the next stile or gate. In summer the ground is generally dry but in autumn and winter, especially because of our climate, the surface can be decidedly wet and slippery; sometimes even glutonous mud!

These comments are part of countryside walking which help to make your walk more interesting or briefly frustrating. Standing in a farmyard up to your ankles in mud might not be funny at the time but upon reflection was one of the highlights of the walk!

ABOUT

JOHN N. MERRILL

John combines the characteristics and strength of a mountain climber with the stamina and athletic capabilities of a marathon runner. In this respect he is unique and has to his credit a whole string of remarkable long walks. He is without question the world's leading marathon walker.

Over the last fifteen years he has walked more than 100,000 miles and successfully completed ten walks of at least 1,000 miles or more.

His six major walks in Great Britain are -
Hebridean Journey.. 1,003 miles
Northern Isles Journey..913 miles
Irish Island Journey... 1,578 miles
Parkland Journey.. 2,043 miles
Lands End to John o'Groats .... 1,608 miles
and in 1978 he became the first person (permanent Guinness Book of Records entry) to walk the entire coastline of Britain — 6,824 miles in ten months.

In Europe he has walked across Austria — 712 miles — hiked the Tour of Mont Blanc, completed High Level Routes in the Dolomites and Italian Alps, and the GR20 route across Corsica in training! In 1982 he walked across Europe — 2,806 miles in 107 days — crossing seven countries, the Swiss and French Alps and the complete Pyrennean chain — the hardest and longest mountain walk in Europe, with more than 600,000 feet of ascent!

In America he used the the world's longest footpath — The Appalachian Trail -2,200 miles — as a training walk. He has walked from Mexico to Canada via the Pacific Crest Trail in record time — 118 days for 2,700 miles. In Canada he has walked the Rideau Trail.

During the summer of 1984, John set off from Virginia Beach on the Atlantic coast, and walked 4,226 miles without a rest day, across the width of America to Santa Cruz and San Francisco on the Pacific Ocean. His walk is unquestionably his greatest achievement, being, in modern history, the longest, hardest crossing of the USA in the shortest time — under six months (178 days). The direct distance is 2,800 miles.

Between major walks John is out training in his own area — the Peak District National Park. As well as walking in other parts of Britain and Europe he has been trekking in the Himalayas five times. He has created more than ten challenge walks which have been used to raise more than £250,000 for charity. From his own walks he raised over £80,000. He is author of more than one hundred books, most of which he publishes himself. His book sales are in excess of 2½ million. He has created many long distance walks including The Limey Way and the Peakalnd Way. He lectures extensively in Britain and America.

CONTENTS

PAGE NO

NARROWBOAT ART

CROSSOVER BRIDGE, MACCLESFIELD CANAL

MARPLE AQUEDUCT

INTRODUCTION

In August 1985 I began walking canal towpaths with the idea of writing a book on them. I soon realised how vast the canal network is and my idea grew to three books, covering my immediate area. Having completed Volume One on the Derbyshire and Nottinghamshire area with more than thirty walks, my aim was to continue where that one left off, but again I underestimnated the scope and now there will be five volumes! For this, Volume Two, I have walked more than 500 miles learning the canal secrets and discovering paths new to me. The attraction of canal walking, to me, lies in the fact that you can see at firsthand a transport system that was the forerunner to our motorway system today.

My aim has simply been to follow each canal from end to end doing a series of walks to illustrate the canal features and surrounding area in which they lie. Whilst you can always return the sameway back along the canal, I wanted to make the vast majority circular to show the canal in its setting. The Macclesfield Canal for instance passes beneath the final Pennine Hills and I have included several walks up in to the hills providing stunning views of the area. One of the joys of canal walking is you don't know what is around the corner—a quiet secluded inn, an old milepost, a series of locks, an aqueduct or a narrowboat cruising along.

This book contains walks which include some of the canals finest architectural and engineering features, built 200 years ago. These include the Marple Aqueduct and flight of locks, the Buxworth Canal Basin, the Bosley Locks, and the Harecastle tunnel. The walks have given me endless pleasure and despite walking for six months experienced no rain! I can only hope that these walks give you an added dimension to exploring the Cheshire and Staffordshire area on foot admidst some fascinating history and scenic beauty.

Happy walking!

John N. Merrill.

JOHN N. MERRILL
Winster. November 1986

TRENT & MERSEY CANAL MILEPOST

MARPLE LOCKS & FORMER WHAREHOUSE

MARPLE AQUEDUCT

PEAK FOREST CANAL

Authorised by Act of Parliament in 1794 the canal was completed, with the exception of the Marple locks in 1800. 14½ miles long from Whaley Bridge to its junction with the Ashton canal at Dunkinfield. The 16 Marple Locks took four years to construct during which time a temporary tramway linked the canal together. The canal engineer was Benjamin Outram, one of the founders of Butterley Ironworks in Derbyshire.

The prime use of the canal was for the transportation of limestone from the Buxton/Doveholes area. The Bugsworth (Buxworth) basin was constructed with tramway from the quarry. Here at Bugsworth stone was either tipped into a boat or lime kiln. The scene was a busy one with boats bringing coal for the kilns. The whole Bugsworth site is particularly interesting and is currently being restored. The Whaley Bridge terminus was linked to the Cromford Canal—engineered by William Jessop and Benjamin Outram in 1794—by the Cromford and High Peak Railway engineered by Josiah Jessop, the son of William, and completed in 1825. There were several schemes for joining the two canals together but because of the hilly terrain of the Peak District, a railway with nine inclines seemed the best practical solution.

The Peak Forest Canal runs through idyllic scenery from the Peak District hills to the fringe of Manchester. The canal is full of features including the 16 locks at Marple and the famous Marple Aqueduct over the river Goyt, 100 feet below. Beyond is the 308 foot long Hyde Bank Tunnel, which has to be walked over as no towpath exists. The Woodley tunnel a little further north is 176 yards long and complete with towpath.

By the middle of the 19th century the canal was losing its trade to the railways and traffic dwindled. Even so Buxworth was still be used until 1922 and the section northwards from Marple Junction was in use until the mid 1930's. The section of the canal from Whaley Bridge towards Marple was still useable in the 1960's but the rest became derelict. Ten years later it had been restored and is now part of the Cheshire Ring.

WOODLEY TUNNEL, PEAK FOREST CANAL

WALK 1—HYDE—4 miles.

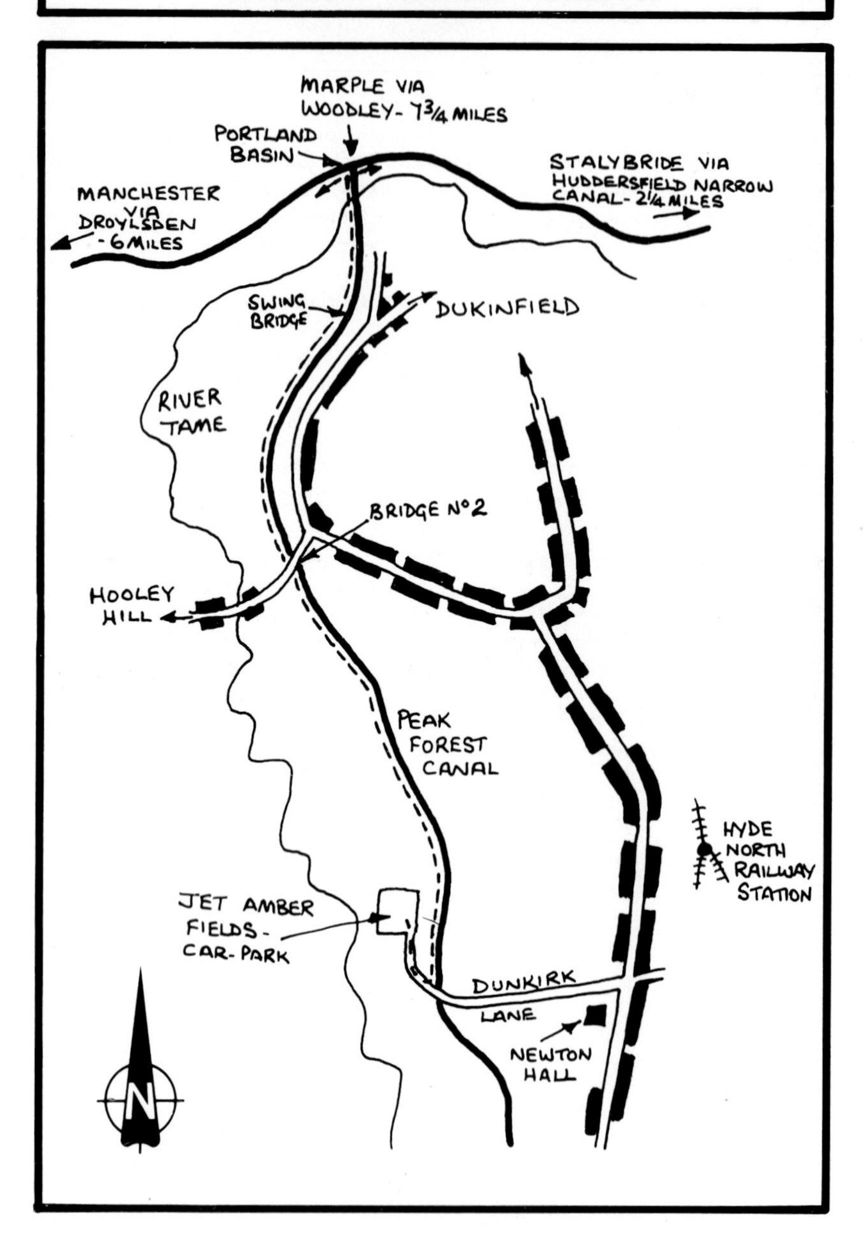

PEAK FOREST CANAL—WALK NO 1—with two extensions—

4 miles—allow 2 hours

ROUTE - Hyde (Jet Amber Fields)—Peak Forest Canal to Portland Basin. Return same way.

MAPS: - O.S. 1:50,000 Sheet No 109—Manchester
—O.S. 1:25,000 Pathfinder Series Sheet No SK89/99 -Manchester and Ashton-under-Lyne.

CAR PARK - Hyde—Jet Amber Fields, beside canal off Dunkirk Lane.

ABOUT THE WALK - Despite the closeness of industry and the suburbia of Manchester, this walk along the northern tip of the canal is extremely pleasant and full of features. You return the sameway but it is again very enjoyable with the Peakland hills in the distance. The climax to the walk is the Portland Basin where the Peak Forest Canal meets the Huddersfield Narrow Canal and the Ashton Canal. From the basin two further walks can be done—one along the Ashton Canal to central Manchester, 6 miles away; and the other along the Huddersfield Narrow Canal to Staylbridge 2 ¼ miles away. Both make enjoyable walks in their own right.

WALKING INSTRUCTIONS - From the car park return along the road to the canal and turn left along it. Keep on it for the next two miles to the Portland Basin, en route passing bridges, a swing bridge and views of the Tame River. Reach the basin at footbridge 30, built in 1835. Here you can extend the walk eastwards to Staylbridge and westwards to Manchester. Retrace your steps back to north Hyde.

FOOTBRIDGE AT PORTLAND BASIN

WALK 2—WOODLEY—4 miles.

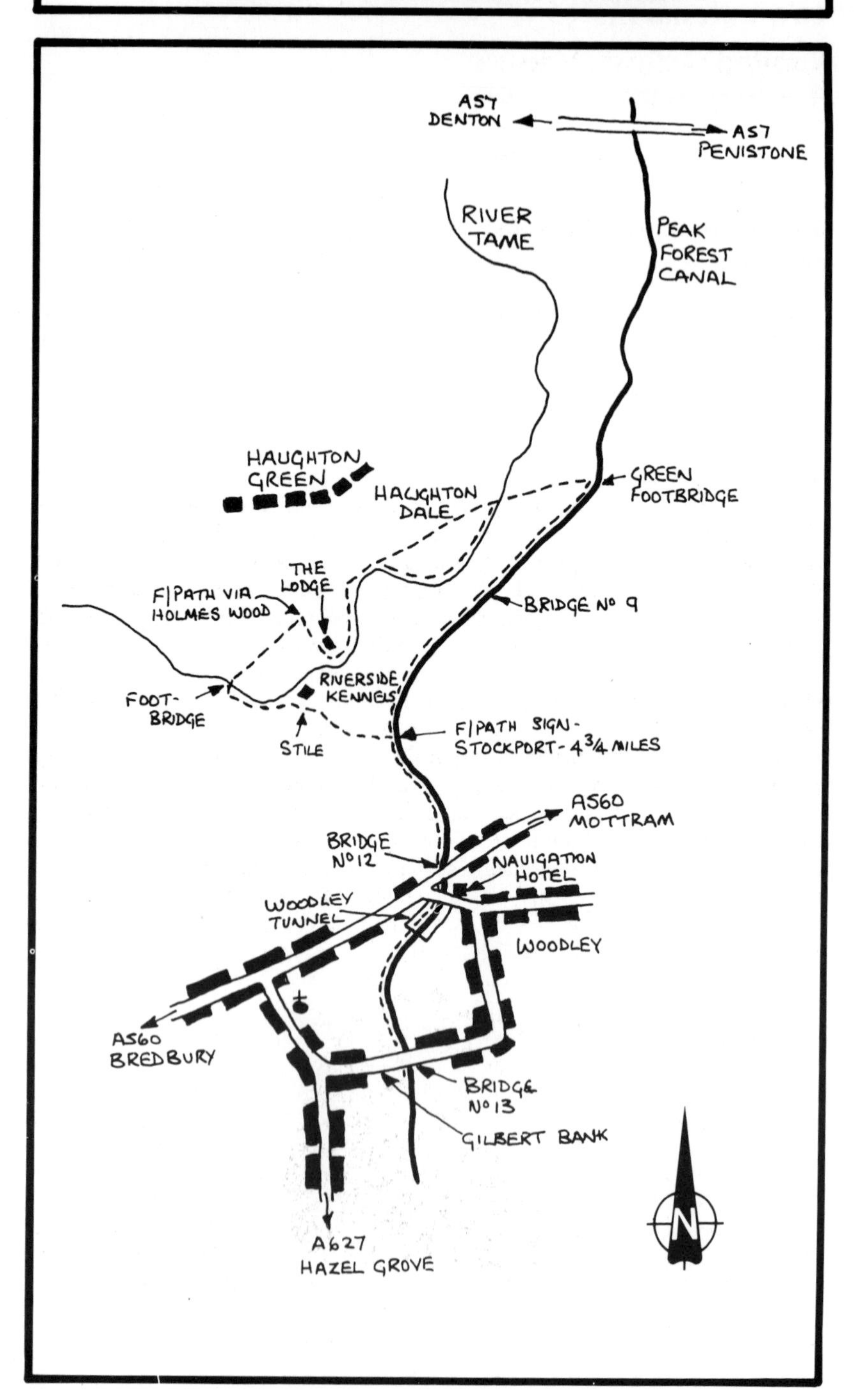

PEAK FOREST CANAL—WALK NO 2

4 miles—allow 2 hours

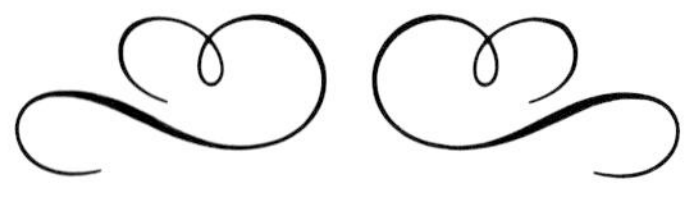

ROUTE - Bridge No 13, south of Woodley—Peak Forest Canal—Haughton Dale and River Tame—Peak Forest Canal—Woodley Tunnel—Bridge No 13.

MAPS: O.S. 1:50,000 Sheet No 109—Manchester
O.S. 1:25,000 Pathfinder Series Sheet No SK89/99—Manchester and Ashton-under-Lyne.

CAR PARK - No official one.

ABOUT THE WALK—I prefer to explore this section of the canal from Bridge 13 as you can walk through, on a towpath, the Woodley Tunnel. You can of course always return the same way on the canal but the adjacent Tame Valley is well worth exploring and is a surprisingly attractive area lying inbetween Stockport and Manchester. Therefore I have made this circular walk to include a section of Tame Valley by walking beside the River Tame and Haughton Dale. There are numerous picnic tables here providing a useful refreshment halt.

WALKING INSTRUCTIONS—Bridge 13 is reached via Gilbert Bank off the A627 in Bredbury—just south of the church. Descend the steps from the bridge to the canal and turn left under the bridge keeping the canal on your right. You keep beside the canal for the next 1 ½ miles. Shortly you walk through the Woodley Tunnel with the Navigation Hotel above before reaching Bridge 12. Beyond this on your left is a path sign—Stockport 4¾ miles. This is the path you will be following to regain the canal after walking beside the River Tame. Keep beside the canal for another ¾ mile, passing Bridge 9, and ¼ mile later reach a green footbridge over the canal. Here turn left and descend the steps and follow the wide path which eventually bears left to a bridge over the River Tame. Cross this and turn left onto the wide path through Haughton Dale. You can keep beside the river or on the path.

After ½ mile ascend steps to approach a group of houses. Bear left still on a path and walk beside the river to the next group of houses—The Lodge. Here walk up the road a little way before turning left, as path signed—Stockport via Hulme Wood. You soon regain the river and cross it via the bridge and turn left on the path. Upon reaching the road to the Riverside Kennels, turn left along it for a few yards to the stile on your right. Turn right through the stile and up the field to the next one. The path line is faint but soon becomes well defined as you follow a fenced path, eventually emerging near a mill on your right. Turn left along the track and regain the canal at the path sign you passed earlier—Stockport 4¾ miles. Turn right and retrace your steps back to Bridge 12, the Woodley Tunnel and Bridge 13.

WALK 3—CHADKIRK—6 miles.

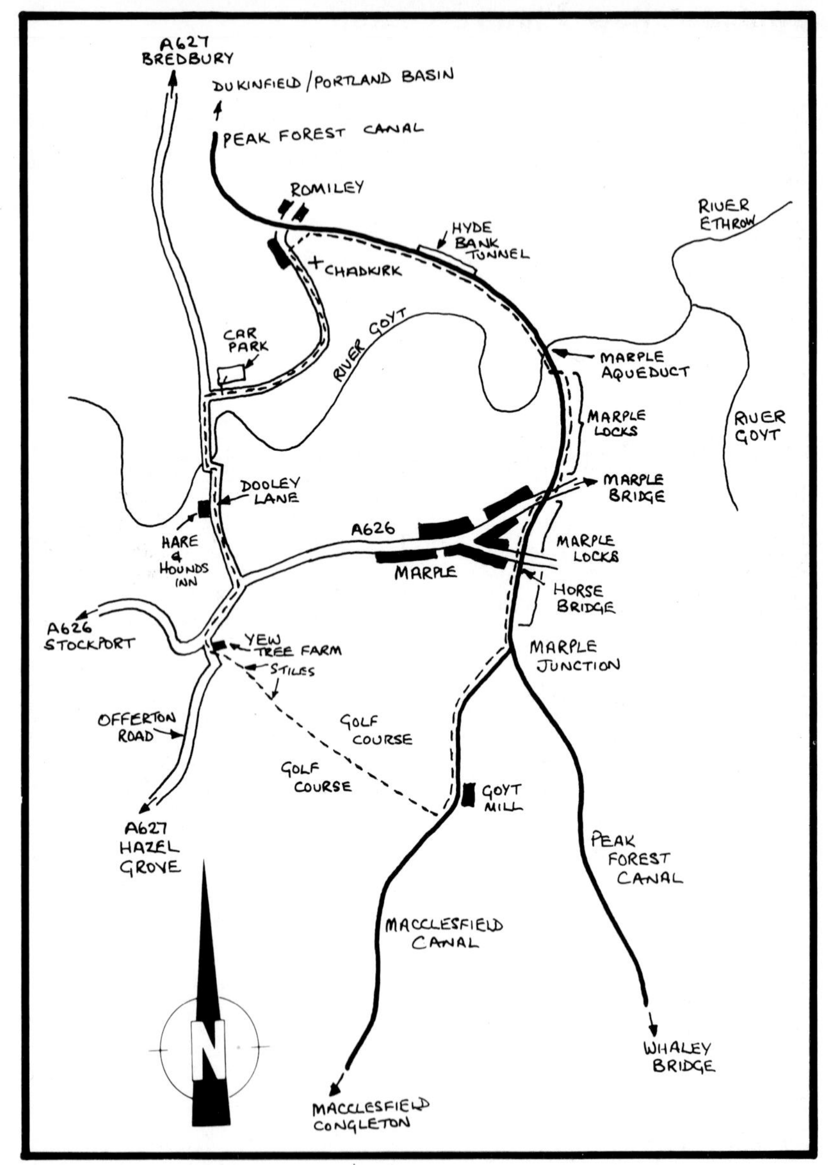

towpath you ascend over it on a defined path then track. Pass Hyde Bank Farm and shortly afterwards, as signposted—Valley Way—descend back to the canal. Continue beside it for a little over ¼ mile and as you near the group of houses just below you on your left, pass through the stone opening and descend to the lane and turn left. You descend to Chadkirk Farm and Chapel and also pick up a Farm Trail. After visiting the chapel continue along the farm drive, bearing right at the bend to reach the car park where you began.

PEAK FOREST CANAL—WALK NO 3

6 miles—allow 2½ to 3 hours.

ROUTE - Chadkirk Car Park—Dooley Lane—Stockport and Marple Golf Course—Macclesfield Canal—Peak Forest Canal—Marple Aqueduct—Chadkirk—Car Park.

MAPS—O.S. 1:50,000 Sheet No 109—Manchester
—O.S. 1:25,000 Pathfinder Series Sheet No SK89/99—Manchester and Ashton-under-Lyne.
—O.S. 1:25,000 Pathfinder Series Sheet No SJ86/96

CAR PARK—Chadkirk, just off A627 road.

ABOUT THE WALK—Following a short road walk and gentle ascent beside golf courses you gain the Macclesfield Canal close to the impressive Goyt Mill. The next four miles can only be described as one of the most fascinating canal walks imaginable. In this short distance you see and pass many of the wonders of the canal era. First the junction of the Peak Forest and Macclesfield canals; then onto a horse tunnel and the sixteen Marple Locks; next is the stunning Marple Aqueduct before the 308 yard long Hyde Bank Tunnel. Shortly afterwards you descend from the canal and pass the historic Chadkirk. It is a walk to savour!

WALKING INSTRUCTIONS—From the car park return to the main road (A627) and turn left along it—Otterspool Road. Follow it over the river Goyt, past a garden centre on your left and the Hare and Hounds Inn on your right. At the junction with the A626 turn right and left shortly afterwards on the A627—Offerton Road. 30 yards later turn left and walk through the farm yard of Yew Tree Farm. Ascend the stile and keep the field boundary on your right, as you follow a track to the next stile. Beyond the trackline leads you closer to the woodland and to a crossroads of paths at a path sign. Here continue ahead—signed Crown Edge and Mellor—and walk beside the woodland for a short distance before entering it and descending the steps and crossing a footbridge. The path is well defined and indicated by yellow arrows and dots, as you ascend gently with the golf course on your right. Eventually cross the disused railway line—now the Middlewood Way—and continue on the edge of the golf course. Further up you cross the fairways to gain the Macclesfield Canal to the right of Goyt Mill, which serves as a good route indicator on this section.

At the canal turn left along it and pass Goyt Mill on your right and later Ring 0' Bells Inn on your right. A little further and you reach the junction of the Macclesfield and Peak Forest Canals. Bear left keeping the canal on your right as you begin descending past the locks and through the horse tunnel. Beyond pass more locks and cross the A626 road bearing right to continue beside the canal—now on your left—as you continue to descend past further locks. After Lock One you cross over to the other side of the canal—now on your right—as you approach the Marple Aqueduct. Continue beside the canal and at the entrance to Hyde Bank Tunnel which has no

WALK 4—MARPLE BRIDGE—6 miles.

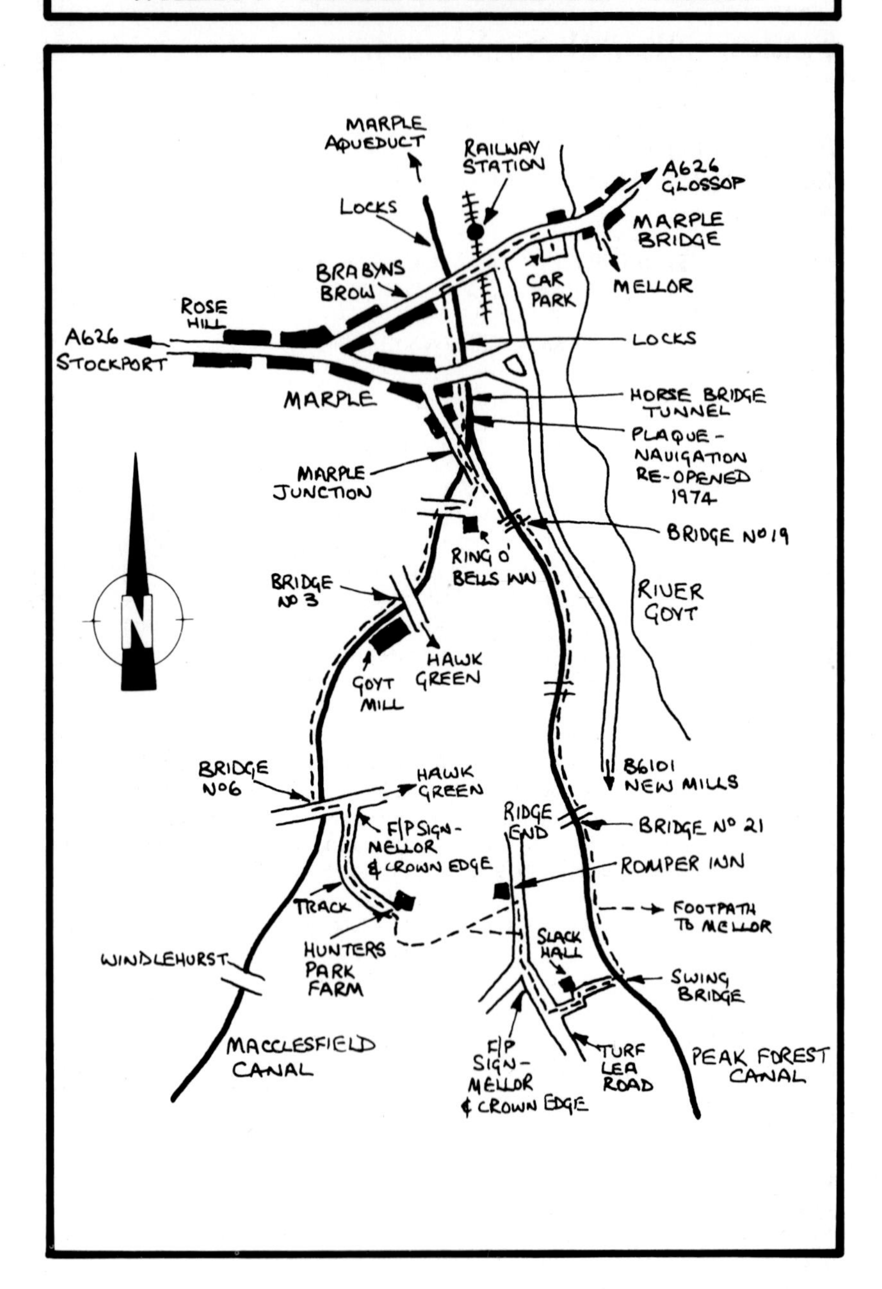

PEAK FOREST CANAL—WALK NO 4

6 miles—allow 2½ hours

ROUTE—Marple Bridge Car Park—Peak Forest Canal—Marple Junction—Macclesfield Canal—Bridge No 6—Romper Inn, Ridge End—Peak Forest Canal—Marple Bridge Car Park.

MAPS—O.S. 1:50,000 Sheet No 109—Manchester
—O.S. 1:25,000 Pathfinder Series Sheet No SJ88/98

CAR PARK—Marple Bridge

ABOUT THE WALK—a short walk that links the Peak Forest and Macclesfield Canals together. First you have a steep walk up the hill from the car park to the Peak Forest Canal, which you follow to the Marple Junction. You follow the Macclesfield Canal from here for a short distance before following paths and tracks to the Peak Forest Canal near Ridge End. Northwards along this returns you past the locks and fascinating horse tunnel back to the road where you began.

WALKING INSTRUCTIONS—Turn left out of the car park and ascend the road to the canal. Turn left and follow it on its righthand side past locks and through the horse tunnel. At the Marple Junction and the start of the Macclesfield Canal cross over the bridge and turn right to the next which you cross to gain the towpath on the canal's righthand side. Follow the canal to Bridge No 6. Here you ascend and cross the bridge to a path sign—Mellor and Cown Edge. Turn right along the track to Hunters Park Farm. Bear right to the fence and turn left along it, keeping it on your righthand side to reach the kissing gate and stiles. At the next track you can keep ahead to the Romper Inn or bear right to the minor road. In both instances you turn right along the road and left along the next one, signed—footpath to Mellor and Cown Edge. Pass Turf Lea Farm and turn left to pass Slack Hall Farm to gain the swing bridge over the Peak Forest Canal. Cross this and turn left keeping the canal on your left. At Bridge No 19 cross the canal and turn right to gain the Marple Junction and bridge you crossed at the beginning. Retrace your steps past the locks on your right and through the horse tunnel back to the A626 road. Turn right and descend back to the car park.

MARPLE LOCKS

WALKS 5,6 & 7—NEW MILLS—4 and 8 miles.

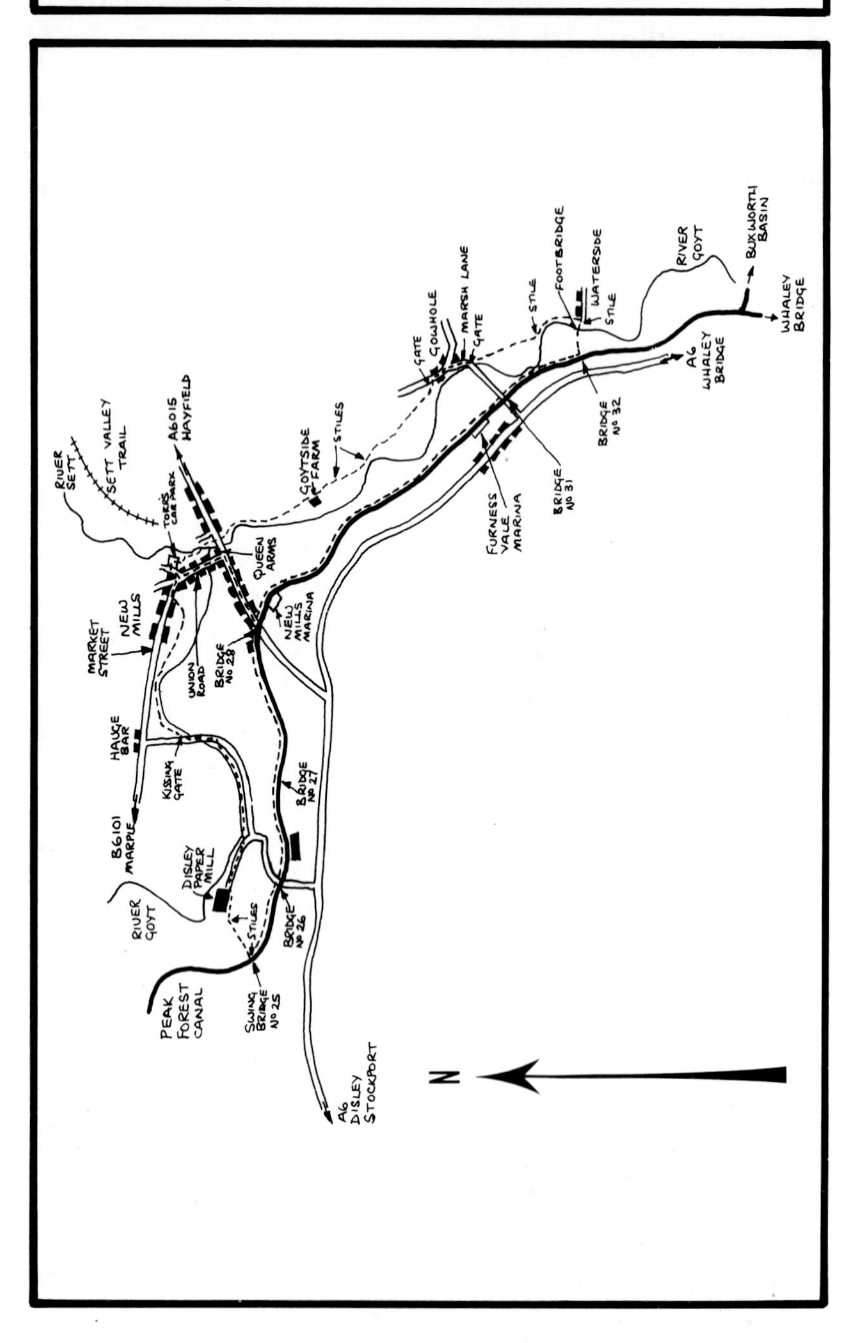

PEAK FOREST CANAL—WALK NOS 5, 6 & 7

4 and 8 miles—allow 2 and 3½ hours

ROUTE—New Mills—Gowhole—River Goyt—Peak Forest Canal—New Mills Marina -Peak Forest Canal—Bridge 25—Disley Paper Mill—Knathole—New Mills.

MAPS—O.S. 1:50,000 Sheet No 109—Manchester
—O.S. 1:50,000 Sheet No 110—Sheffield and Huddersfield
—O.S. 1:25,000 Outdoor Leisure Map—The Dark Peak
—O.S. 1:25,000 Pathfinder Series Sheet Nos SJ88/98 and SK08/18

CAR PARK—New Mills—Torr Top Street

ABOUT THE WALK—The walk can be either 4, 6 or 8 miles long—as you can either do the whole circuit or the western or the eastern loop, using New Mills as the break point. All walks include a major section of the canal with a walk close to the River Goyt. The walking is particularly attractive with the Pennine hills around you as the canal nears its southern end at Whaley Bridge. Much of the walking is along quiet paths and beside an unspoilt canal.

WALKING INSTRUCTIONS—From the car park descend the signposted path—The Torrs—and turn right at junction to keep on The Torrs path; to your left is the Sett Valley Trail. Keep on the path and pass under the road bridge following the path signed—Gowhole. At first you are close to the River Goyt on your right before the fenced track heads for Goytside Farm. Keep straight ahead at the farm on the defined path for Gowhole a mile away. Upon reaching the road at Gowhole-Marsh Lane—turn right and, just before the bridge over the River Goyt, left through the path gate and cross the field to stone stile. Continue across the next field—the path line is not obvious, being little used, but the stile ahead is a good guide. At the end of the next field you regain the river before heading for the houses of Waterside with a stile at the righthand house. On gaining the end of the road turn right to another stile and cross a footbridge and ascend two fields on a defined path to gain the Peak Forest canal at Bridge 32. Turn right and follow the canal for the next 3½ miles.

PEAK FOREST CANAL NEAR HYDE

On the way pass Furness Vale Marina on your left after ½ a mile and 1½ miles further New Mills Marina. Here you can leave the canal by turning right to the A6015 road and by following this for ¼ mile to the Queen Arms. Turn left up Union Road to regain the car park at the top, on your right where you started.

Those on the complete circuit keep on the towpath and pass under Bridge 28 and continue for 1⅓ miles to Swing Bridge No 25. Opposite on your right is the stile and steps. Descend these and continue ahead in woodland descending and crossing a small stream before gaining a wooden stile before Disley Paper Mill. Turn right through the mill on the road and ascend the road a short distance to a stile on your left and the path to Waterside. There is an earlier path with footbridges but this loops round to this path. The path is well defined and upon reaching the road turn left and cross the River Goyt Bridge to reach a kissing gate on your right. Turn right along the path to another gate and onto another stile. After this you leave the river and begin ascending on a defined path with views of New Mills and pass through a pic-nic area before descending to Knothole. Turn left at the road and follow it as it ascends past New Mills Central station to Market Street. Turn right and at the top of Union Road a few yards later bear half left along Back Union Road to reach the car park.

As you will have seen, there are several other walks starting from New Mills, including the 3 mile Sett Valley Trail and a 2 mile Torrs Bridges Trail—both are highly recommended.

PEAK FOREST CANAL IN NEW MILLS

FURNESS VALE MARINA, PEAK FOREST CANAL

CHADKIRK

WALK 8—WHALEY BRIDGE—2 miles.

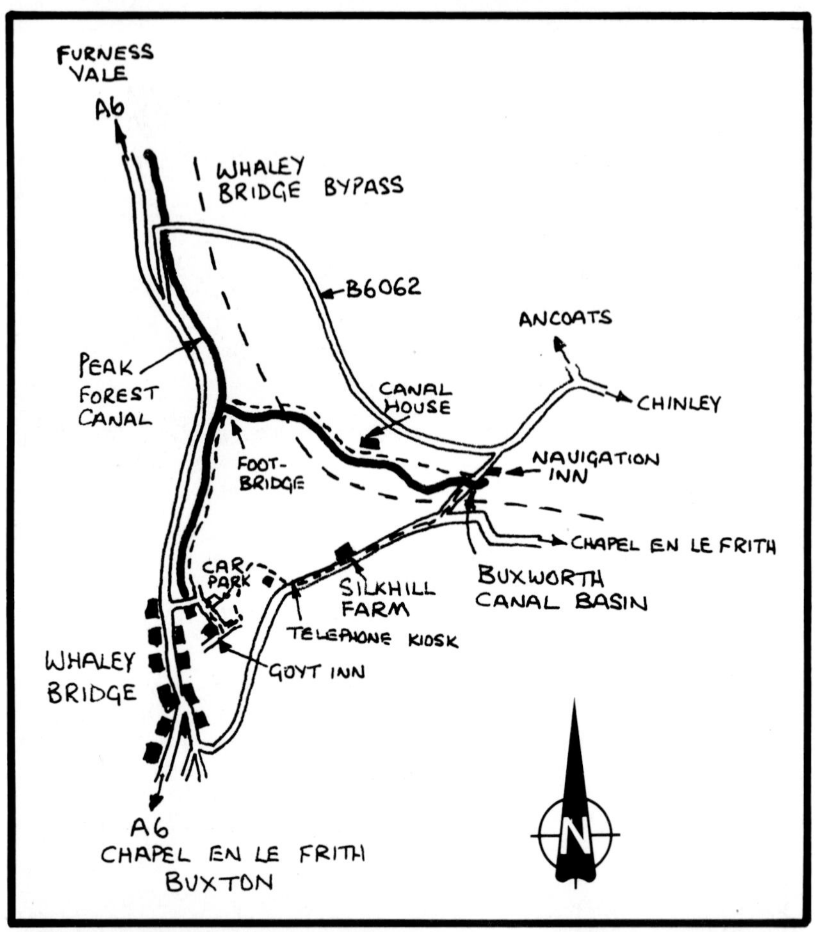

PEAK FOREST CANAL AT WHALEY BRIDGE

PEAK FOREST CANAL—WALK NO 8

2 miles—allow one hour

ROUTE—Whaley Bridge—Silkhill Farm—Buxworth—Peak Forest Canal—Whaley Bridge.

MAPS: O.S. 1:25,000 Outdoor Leisure Map—The Dark Peak
O.S. 1:25,000 Pathfinder Series Sheet No SK08/18

CAR PARK—Whaley Bridge, close to start of Peak Forest Canal.

ABOUT THE WALK—a very short one with a pub half-way! The attraction of the route lies in seeing the Buxworth (Bugsworth) canal basin, which in late 1986 is being restored. Here you can imagine the busy scene of loading the canal boats before they began their journey. You descend the arm of the basin to the Peak Forest canal and follow it back to its end at Whaley Bridge. A very historical circuit and one not to be hurried!

WALKING INSTRUCTIONS—Turn left out of the car park and walk past the houses to the road beside the Goyt Inn. Turn left and cross the River Goyt before turning left and following the path above the river with the site of Goyt Mill on your right. After 200 yards the path—a tarmaced one—leaves the river and begins ascending to the Buxworth road, in the final stages passing a farm and at the road a telephone kiosk on your left. Turn left and follow the ascending road past Silkhill Farm and descend to Buxworth Basin and the Navigation Inn. Turn left and follow the track past the Canal House and on under the bypass to the Peak Forest Canal. Turn left over the footbridge and continue beside the canal on your right back to Whaley Bridge.

BUGSWORTH CANAL BASIN

WALK 9—END TO END WALK—14¾ miles .

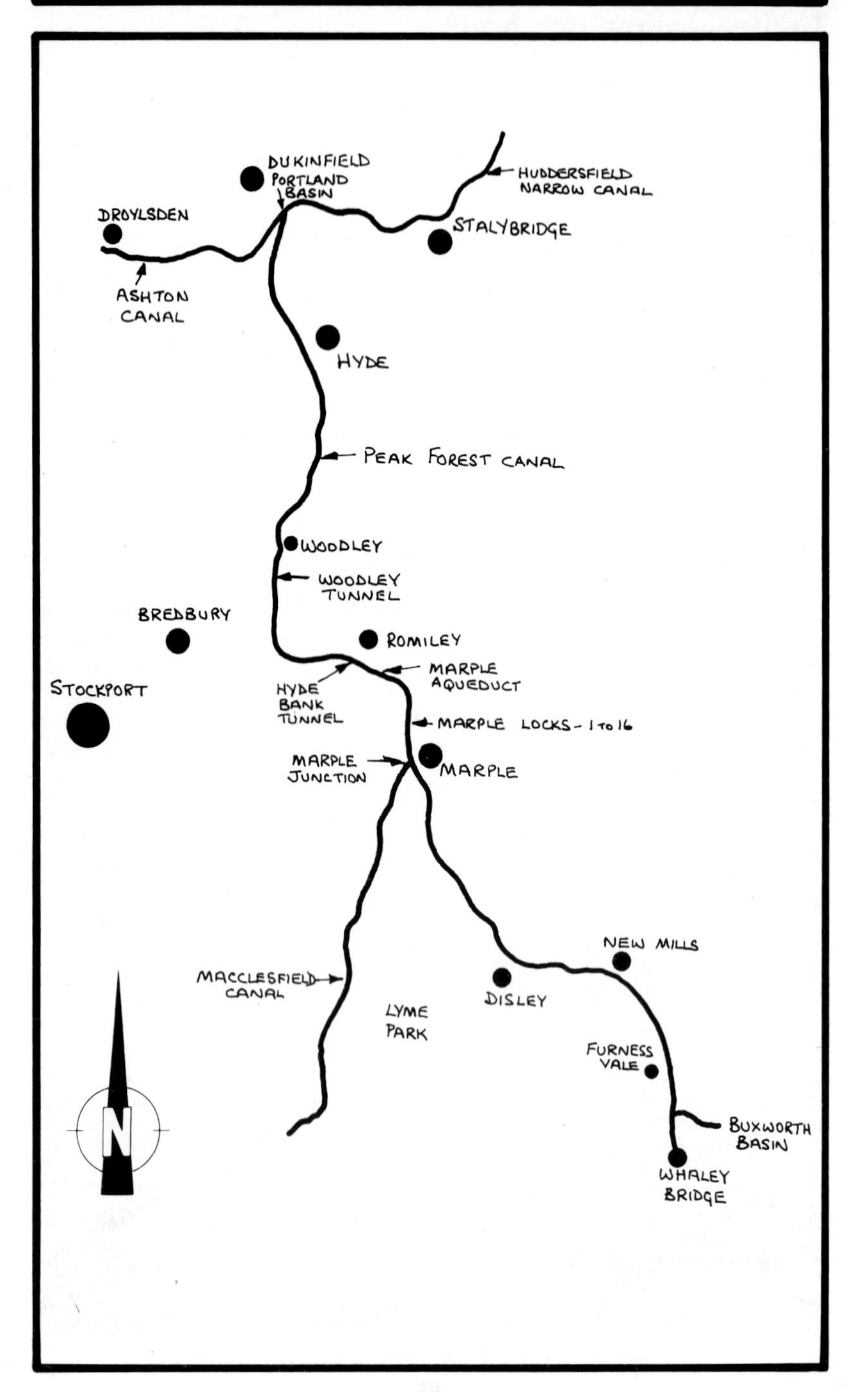

PEAK FOREST CANAL—END TO END—14¾ miles—allow 6 hours

MAPS—O.S. 1:50,000 Sheet No 110—Sheffield and Huddersfield
—O.S. 1:50,000 Sheet No 109—Manchester

ABOUT THE WALK—Starting from Whaley Bridge, following the length of the canal to the Portland Basin at Dukinfield is a particularly attractive walk—from the Pennines to the city. There are car parks at either end. Whilst it makes a splendid one-way walk, Marple is basically the halfway point—7¾ miles from the Portland Basin—and can therefore be used to do two shorter walks on the canal—one Marple to Whaley Bridge and the other Marple to the Portland Basin. You can always return the same way, making a round trip of approximately 15 miles each. You will be surprised how different a place looks from the opposite direction!

PORTLAND BASIN

PEAK FOREST CANAL—WHALEY BRIDGE

MACCLESFIED CANAL NEAR CONGLETON

MACCLESFIELD CANAL

MACCLESFIELD CANAL

Authorised by Act in 1826 it was fully operational in 1831 and is 27¾ miles long with 13 locks. The basic line was surveyed by Thomas Telford but the canal engineer was William Crosley. The canal joins the Peak Forest Canal near Marple in the north and leaves the Trent & Mersey at Hardings Wood Junction near Kidsgrove. The canal forms part of the 90 mile Cheshire Ring, to be dealt with in a future volume.

The canal is one of the most attractive passing beneath the final hills of the Pennines, where the Cheshire Plain begins. Basically on a south to north axis the canal passes Congleton and through Macclesfield and Bollington following a largely straight course, with impressive embankments and aqueducts, especially at Bollington and Hardings Wood. The canal does a sharp turn at Bosley where twelve locks are located with the rocky hill of The Cloud standing guard.

Although one of the last canals to be constructed the canal saw extensive use in the 19th century despite competition from the railways—the canal was bought by the Great Central Railway Company, who also purchased the Peak Forest and Ashton canals. By the end of the century like all canals traffic had steadily declined. This century saw its continued decline and as the Peak Forest and Ashton canals were out of use, the Macclesfield Canal was no longer a through route. In the 1960's it was little used but a decade later with the restoration of the Peak Forest and Ashton canals the canal has been transformed into one of the most interesting. The Macclesfield Canal also has the honour of being the first canal to have a canal boat club—the North Cheshire Cruising Club—founded in 1943.

BOSLEY LOCKS

WALK 1—POYNTON COPPICE—5 miles.

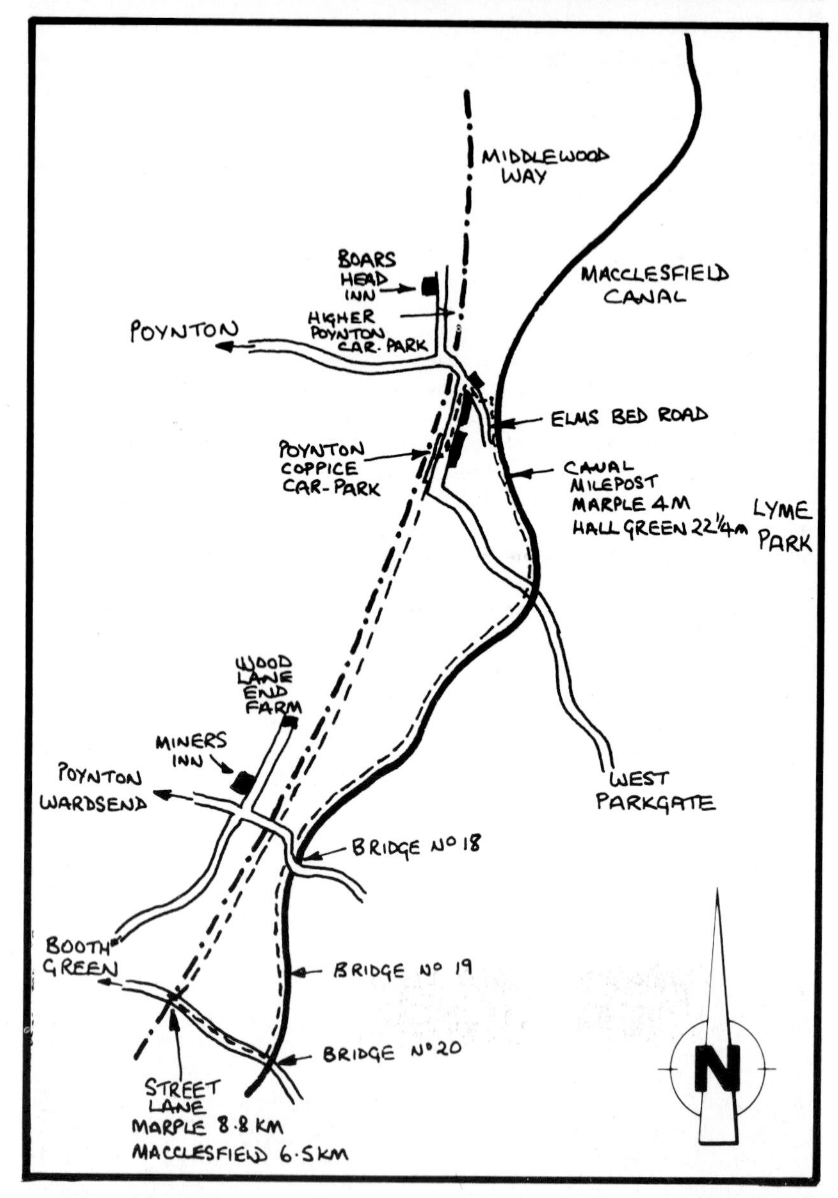

THE MIDDLEWOOD WAY—11 miles from Marple to Macclesfield. A former railway line—the M,B and M railway (Macclesfield, Bollington and Marple.) Built in the 1860's it was never a great success and in 1970 it was closed to both passenger and goods trains. The Macclesfield Borough and Stockport Metropolitan Borough Councils worked together to change the line to a leisureway for walkers, cyclists and riders, and it was opened in 1985.

MACCLESFIELD CANAL—WALK NO 1

5 miles—allow 2½ hours

ROUTE—Poynton Coppice Car Park—Macclesfield Canal—Bridge 20—Middlewood Way—Poynton Coppice Car Park.

MAPS—O.S.—1:50,000 Sheet No 109—Manchester
—O.S.—1:25,000 Pathfinder Series Sheet No SJ88/98

ABOUT THE WALK—First you walk along one of the quieter and unspolit sections of the Macclesfield Canal before returning to your starting point via the Middlewood Way. Historically it is interesting to see the canal—the forerunner of transport before the advent of railways. Perhaps there is poetic justice for the railway has now gone whilst the canal, although rarely used for transporting goods or materials, is still used by narrowboats. The Middlewood Way runs close to the canal and although I have detailed only one walk here there is ample scope to do several others using the "way" to create circular routes of varying lengths.

WALKING INSTRUCTIONS—From the car park return to the minor road and turn left and follow it past the houses to the sharp lefthand bend. Here on your right is Elm Beds Road. Turn right along this for a few yards to the stile and fenced path on your left. Follow this to the edge of the playing field and steps to the canal. Turn right along the canal and soon pass milestone—Hall Green 22¼ miles and Marple 4 miles. You now follow the canal southwards for the next two miles to Bridge 20—you know you have walked too far if you reach the canal milepost stating—Hall Green 20¼ miles and Marple 6 miles!

Ascend to road heading westwards to the Middlewood Way and descend to the "way". The bridge bears the sign—Street Lane, Marple 8.8 Km, Macclesfield 6.5 Km. You now head northwards along the path for two miles back to the car park. To the left of the second bridge is the Miners Inn.

MIDDLEWOOD WAY

WALK 2—BOLLINGTON—6 miles.

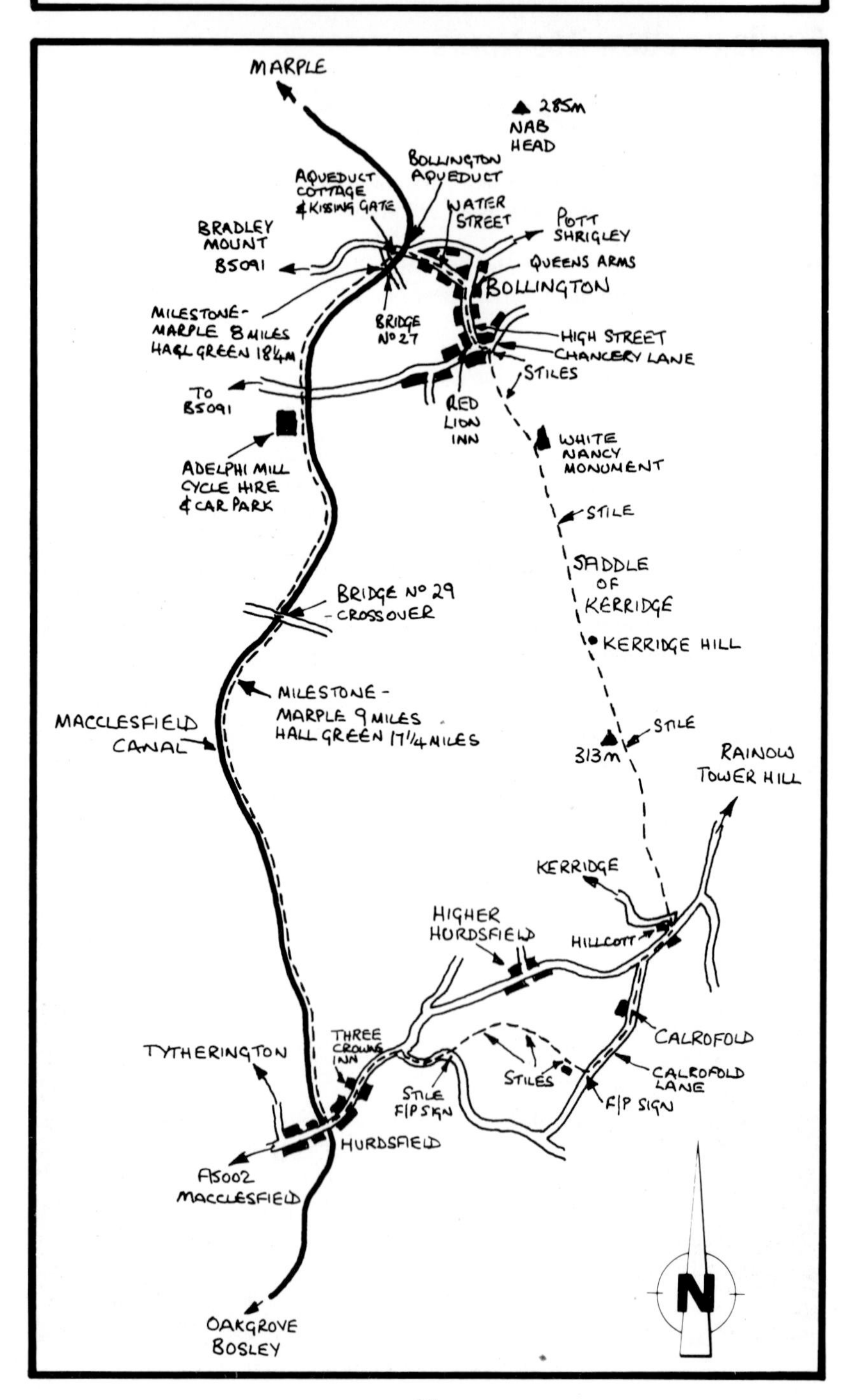

MACCLESFIELD CANAL—WALK No 2

6 miles—allow 2½ hours

ROUTE—Bollington—White Nancy—Kerridge Hill—Tower Hill—Calrofold—Higher Hurdsfield—Macclesfield Canal—Bollington.

MAPS—O.S. 1:50,000 Sheet No 118—The Potteries
—O.S. 1:25,OOO Pathfinder Series Sheet No SJ 87/97—Macclesfield & Alderley Edge.

CAR PARK—Adelphi Mill, Bollington.

ABOUT THE WALK—I prefer to start this walk from Water Street as you do not see the canal until later. The Macclesfield Canal passes beneath the final slopes of the Pennines at the foot of the Cheshire Plain. This walk combines both to appreciate the canal's setting and one of the finest vantage points on the fringe of the Peak District National Park. The walk has a little of everything—steep ascent (at the start), distant views, attractive hamlets and farms, the tranquil and flat canal walking, and the large buildings and chimneys of the mills that populate the area. The canal travels high above the village across two impressive aqueducts.

WALKING INSTRUCTIONS—Starting from Water Street, walk along the road away from the large aqueduct. «If starting from Adelphi Mill, ascend to canal and turn left and walk beside the canal for ¼ mile passing bridge No 27 and Milestone—Marple 8 miles, Hall Green 18 ¼ miles. Just afterwards leave the canal at the kissing gate near Aqueduct Cottage, with a timber yard on the other side of the canal. Turn right in front of the cottage and descend steeply to the road. Turn right and pass under the aqueduct and right into Water Street.—Those starting from Water Street will do this at the end of the walk.»

BOLLINGTON AQUEDUCT, MACCLESFIELD CANAL

Walk up Water Street to its end opposite the Queen's Arms and turn right into High Street and follow this to its junction with Chancery Lane and Red Lion Inn. Turn left then right at the stile and footpath sign beside the last house and ascend gradually with the field boundary on your right. At the next stile pass through it and bear left before ascending again more steeply. Just over the brow gain a cross roads of paths. Continue ahead ascending to the white monument on White Nancy. The view is exceptional over the Cheshire Plain, Jodrell Bank and Manchester Airport. For the next 1½ miles you basically keep to the crest of the Saddle of Kerridge, gaining a trig point after a mile. The path shortly afterwards bears left beside some quarries on your right to a stile. Over this you continue descending gently to a minor road, opposite the house named "Hillcott". Turn left to the A5002 road.

Turn right and shortly afterwards left into Calrofold Lane. Follow this for a little over ¼ mile to a path sign on your right and walk up the house drive and past the building on your right to a stile and steps on your left. First you keep the wall on your right, and after the first stile it is on your left. The path is well stiled as you curve round the hillside and gain a minor road via a stile beside a path sign. Turn right and follow round to your left—Cliff Lane to the A5002 road in Higher Hurdsfield. Turn left and the canal is ¼ mile away, gained on your left. On the way pass an old milestone, white painted—Macclesfield 1 mile—and the Three Crowns Inn on your right.

Gain the canal and turn right, and for the next mile the towpath keeps to the righthand side. On the way pass a canal milestone—Marple 9 miles, Hall Green 17¼ miles. At bridge No 29—a cross over bridge—you cross to the lefthand side of the canal and just over a mile later you are back into Bollington, with the Adelphi Mill on your left and the aqueduct and Water Street, ¼ mile further.

MACCLESFIELD CANAL MILEPOST

BOLLINGTON—dominated by the 1,000 foot high ridge of Kerridge, the town had numerous mills, driven by the many streams and later by coal carried on the canal. The last cotton mill ceased operating in 1960. The Kerridge Hill has the reknowned landmark—White Nancy. This is believed to have been built by the Gaskell family to commemorate the Battle of Waterloo, and Nancy was a member of the family. The houses are built from stone quarried from the Kerridge Hill.

MACCLESFIELD CANAL

CROSSOVER BRIDGE, MACCLESFIELD CANAL

WALKS 3,4,5 & 6—MACCLESFIELD—4 miles

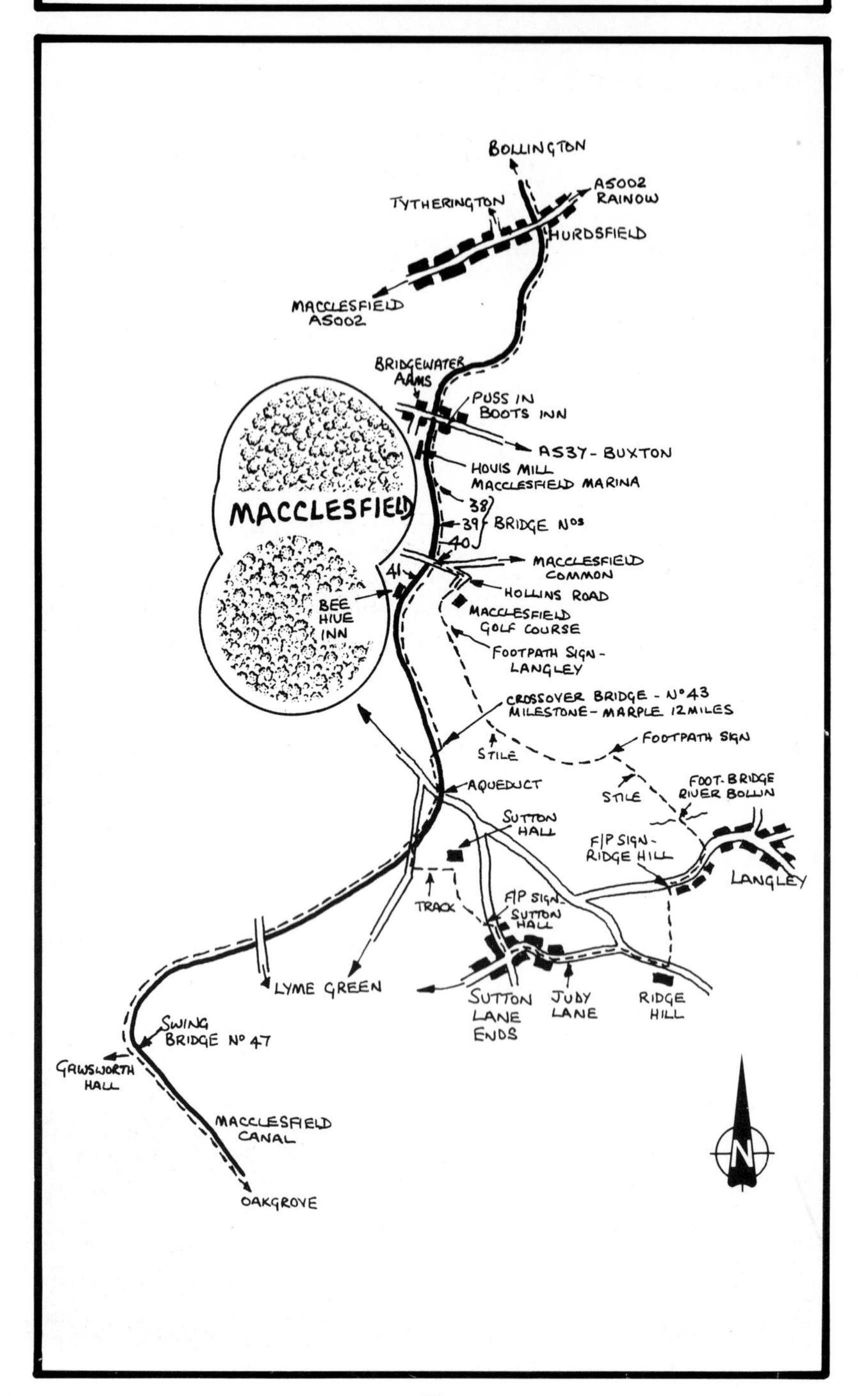

MACCLESFIELD CANAL—WALK NOS 3, 4, 5, & 6

4 miles—allow 2 hours

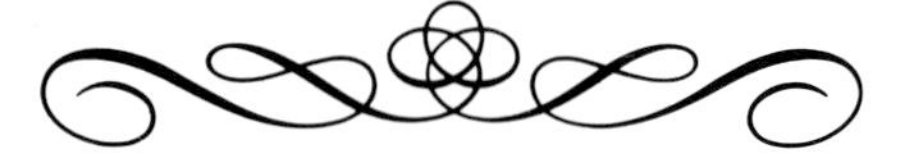

ROUTE—Macclesfield (Hollins Road)—Golf Course—River Bollin—Langley—Ridge Hill—Sutton Lane Ends—Sutton Hall—Macclesfield Canal—Macclesfield (Hollins Road).

CAR PARK—No official one.

MAPS—O.S. 1:25,000 Pathfinder Series Sheet No SJ87/97 and SJ86/96.

ABOUT THE WALK—a magnificent walk, illustrating the setting of the canal on the eastern edge of the town with the Peak District hills and Macclesfield Forest close by. Macclesfield serves as an important centre for exploring this area of the canal, and although there are few paths enabling you to do longer circuits, it is possible to return walk along the canal from Hollins Road and link in with other walks that are detailed. As a result there are four different walks from here, but first the main one.

WALKING INSTRUCTIONS—From bridge 40—Hollins Road—continue ascending, bearing right up Hollins Road and following it round to your right past the Macclesfield Golf Course Clubhouse. The road is now a track, and after 100 yards as stiled and footpath signed on your left—Langley—turn left and follow the well- defined path. First around the golf course and past a concrete reservoir on your left. Ahead can be seen the Peakland Hills and Macclesfield Forest, while to your right is the canal below and the Cheshire Plain. The path contours round for another ½ mile to a path sign in memory of Mable Lake. Here turn right—Langley—and begin descending first to a stile and then to a footbridge over the infant River Bollin. A little further and gain the minor road with Langley to your left.

ADELPHI MILL, BOLLINGTON

Turn right and walk beside the road for 200 yards to the path sign on your left—Ridgehill— with Ridgewood House on your right. Ascend the field gaining the minor road opposite Ridge Hill. Turn right and take the first lane on your left—Judy Lane- just after a pig farm on your left. Descend the lane towards Sutton Lane Ends, bearing left along Church Lane. At the cross roads in the village turn right along Hall Lane and after a few yards left at the path sign—Sutton Hall—opposite Beck Cottage. The path keeps near a stream to a stile before you cross a large field to its far lefthand corner. Sutton Hall is just ahead on your right. Turn left at the stile and walk along the track to a minor road and path sign. Turn right past the entrance to Sutton Hall and onto the bridge over the canal—roadside parking here. Turn right onto the towpath and head northwards with the canal on your right.

About 200 yards later pass canal milepost—Marple 12 miles—and gain bridge 43 and cross over to the other side of the canal on the crossover bridge. Continue ahead with the canal now on your left and almost a mile later pass the Bee Hive Inn on the other side of the canal! before reaching Bridge 40. Pass under it before taking the path on your right to Hollins Road. But before doing so it is very worthwhile walking another ½ mile to see the Macclesfield Marina and Hovis Mill. Retrace your steps back to Bridge 40 and Hollins Road.

OTHER WALKS—Using Hollins Road and Bridge 40 as a base you can do three other walks from here.

1. Northwards along the canal to Hurdsfield and joining the Bollington/ Kerridge walk, No 2 this adds approximately 2½ miles to the circuit and you retrace your steps back to Bridge 40.
2. Southwards along the canal to Oakgrove—about 5½ mile return walk.
3. Southwards to join the Gawsworth Hall circuit, Walk No 8 and this extends the walk by 4 miles including retracing your steps back to Bridge 40.

MACCLESFIELD CANAL MILEPOST

MACCLESFIELD (centre)—ten minutes from Bridge No 37 is the Heritage Centre and Paradise Mill. Silk weaving was the principal industry here from 1750 onwards. The last handloom buisness ceased in 1981. Paradise Mill, a Victorian Silk Mill, has been reopened as a working museum and is open most days.

MACCLESFIELD MARINA AND FORMER HOVIS MILL

NARROWBOATS AT MACCLESFIELD MARINA

WALK 7—OAKGROVE—5 miles.

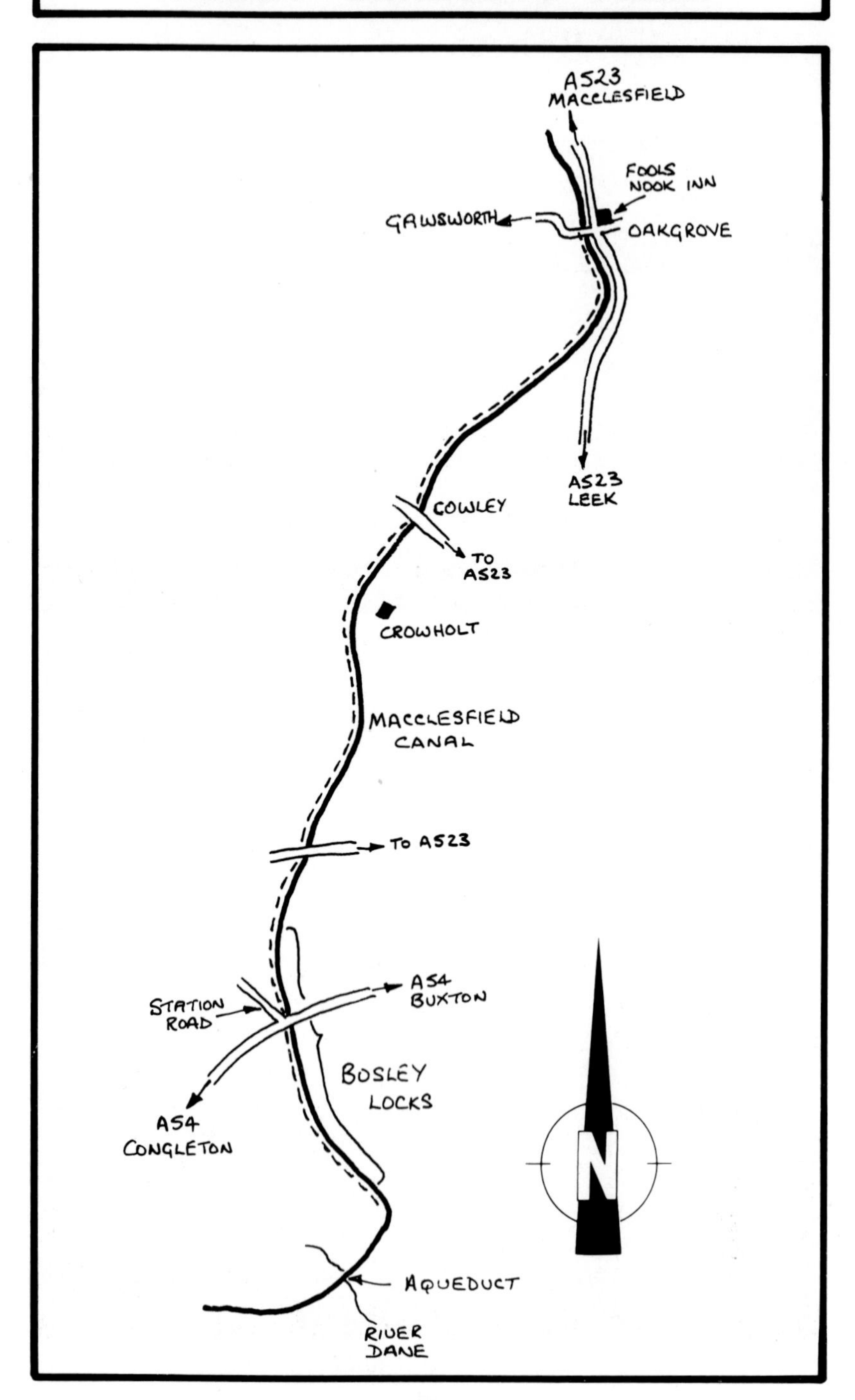

MACCLESFIELD CANAL—WALK NO 7

5 miles—allow 2½ hours

ROUTE—Oakgrove—Macclesfield Canal—Bosley Locks. return same way.

MAPS—O.S. 1:50,000 Sheet No 118—The Potteries
-O.S. 1:25,000 Pathfinder Series Sheet No SJ 86/96—Congleton

CAR PARK—No official one at Oakgrove.

ABOUT THE WALK—A return walk along the towpath between the swing-bridge at Oakgrove, near Fools Nook Inn, to the Bosley Locks. There are no other rights of way in this area; hence a return walk. The canal is particularly attractive along this stretch and the Bosley Locks are an interesting feature, especially when a narrow boat is negotiating the numerous locks.

WALKING INSTRUCTIONS—At the swing bridge turn right along the towpath on the right of the canal. Keep beside the canal for the next 2½ miles to the Bosley Locks. You can extend the walk by following the locks round for ½ mile or even do another of the walks—Nos 9 & 10—which start from here! Return northwards along the canal back to Oakgrove.

BOSLEY LOCKS

WALK 8—OAKGROVE/GAWSWORTH HALL—4½ miles.

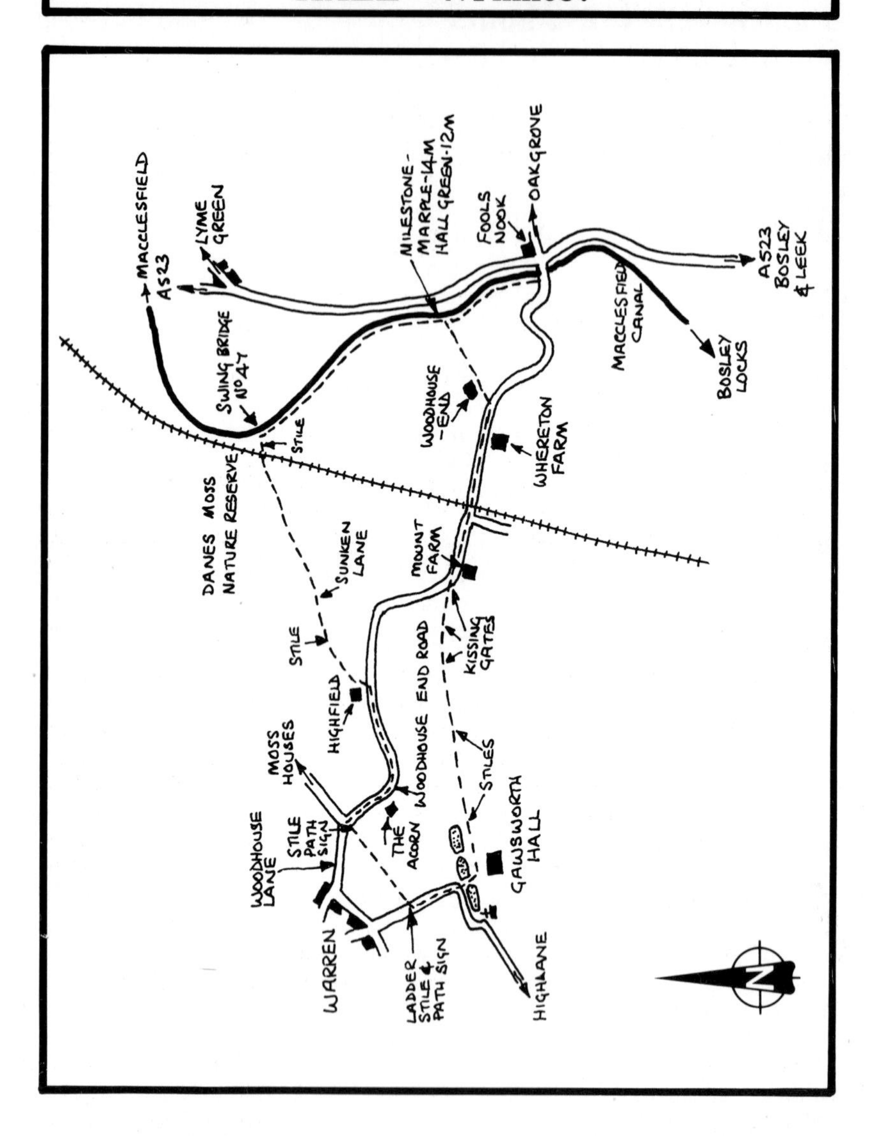

GAWSWORTH HALL—The hall and church date from Norman times but the current buildings date from the 15th century. The hall was built by the Fitton family who were reknown for their jousting. The grounds include one of the finest tilting arenas in England—200 yards long by 60 yards wide. Members of the family include Mary Fytton, known as the "Dark Lady" of Shakespeare's Sonnets. The hall is open to the public and the church is located above one of the five ponds and is particularly attractive.

MACCLESFIELD CANAL—WALK NO 8

4½ miles—allow 2 hours—more if visiting Gawsworth Hall.

ROUTE—Oakgrove—Macclesfield Canal—Bridge 47—Danes Moss Nature Reserve—Gawsworth—Mount Farm—Macclesfield Canal—Oakgrove.

MAPS—0.S. 1:50,000 Sheet No 118—The Potteries
—O.S. 1:25,000 Pathfinder Series Sheet No SJ 86/96—Congleton
—O.S. 1:25,000 Pathfinder Series Sheet No SJ 87/97—Macclesfield & Alderley Edge

CAR PARK—No official one at Oakgrove.
—Hall car park at Gawsworth.

ABOUT THE WALK—First you follow a small section of the canal before leaving it to walk through Danes Moss Nature Reserve. A mile later you reach Gawsworth with its magnificent hall—open to the public—impressive church and series of ponds. You return across the fields and minor road to the canal which you follow back to Oakgrove.

WALKING INSTRUCTIONS—At the swing-bridge turn left along the canal towpath, with the canal on your right. You keep on the canal for the next mile. After ¼ mile you pass a canal milepost—Marple 14 miles/Hall Green 12 miles. Just past it on your left is a path and steps; it is up these you will be ascending on your return from Gawsworth. Keep beside the canal for another ¾ mile to Swing Bridge No 47. Here turn left through the stile and cross the railway line—with caution—and follow the well defined path through Danes Moss Nature Reserve. Little over ½ mile from the railway line gain a path crossroads. Keep ahead to stile and now on a faint path keep the field boundary on your right to the house and corner of the field. Turn left still following the field boundary to the road. Turn right and pass Highfield House. Keep on the road—Woodhouse End Road—for almost ½ mile to a road junction, on the outskirts of Warren village and the start of Woodhouse Lane. Turn left as footpath signed and cross the fields on a defined path to the Gawsworth Road. Turn left into Gawsworth.

At the entrance to the hall, on your right is the car park and minor road past the ponds to the church. Keep ahead towards the hall and follow the road round to your right, passing two ponds. At the end of the last one pass through a stile and continue across the field with the field boundary on your right. The path has several wooden kissing gates before gaining the minor road near Mount Farm. Bear right along the road past the farm and over the railway line and past Whereton Farm on your right. 100 yards later on your left is the track to Woodhouse-end and path sign. Turn left up here to the farm. Entering turn right and walk round the farm before descending the field to a footbridge over a stream. Beyond ascend the steps to regain the canal close to the milepost you passed earlier. Turn right and walk back along the canal to Oakgrove, the swing bridge and Fools Nook Inn.

WALK 9 & 10—BOSLEY/THE CLOUD–4 & 9 miles.

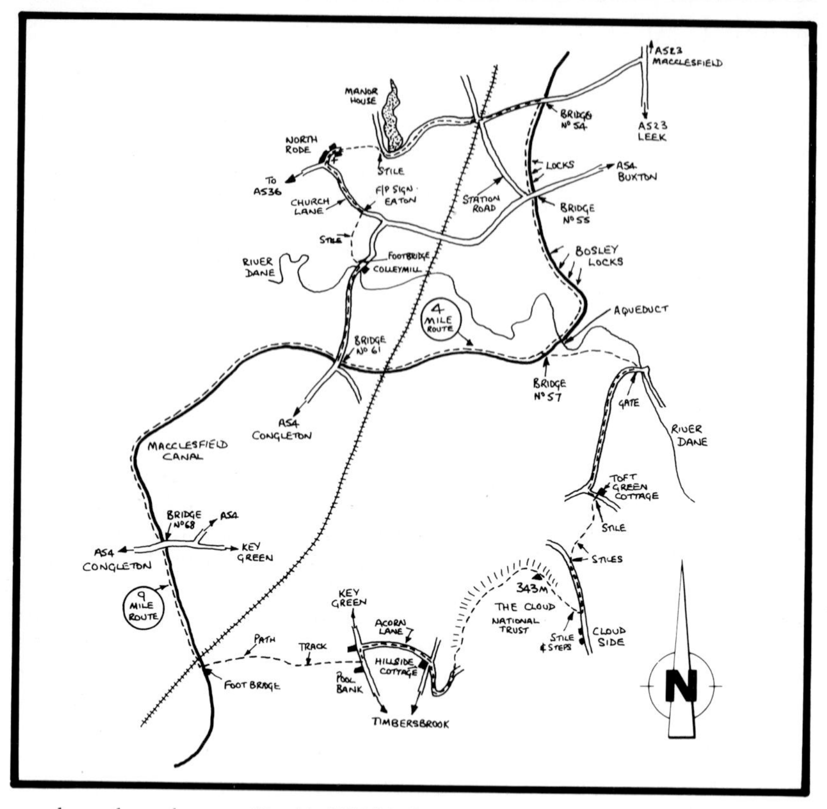

reach another minor road beside Hillside Cottage. Cross to your right and ascend the lane which soon swings left. Here you leave it and follow the wide path beside the National Trust sign, The Cloud. Continue ascending to the trees. Don't follow the path in them but turn left and keep in open country as you gradually ascend on a footpath to the trig point on the summit of The Cloud. Follow the path round to a stile and bear left down the steps to the minor road and turn left.

After about 200 yards descent take the second stile on your right well before the first house on your right, and cross the field to the right of it to a stile. Descend the next field, aiming for the solitary house—Toft Green Cottage. The pathline is non-existent here. Ascend the stile and turn left in front of the cottage and gain the minor road. Turn right and follow it downhill for over ½ mile, almost to the River Dane. Just before it go through the gate on your left. Again this right of way is little used but a grass track guides you across the field to a stile beside the trees, with the river a little to your right. Bear left to another stile and ascend afterwards on a path to another. In the next field bear left to bridge No 57 over the canal. On your right and what you will be walking along next is the aqueduct over the River Dane. Descend to the towpath and follow it to your right over the aqueduct and to the Bosley Locks. Walk beside them to the A54 road ½ mile away.

MACCLESFIELD CANAL—WALK NOS 9 and 10

4 and 9 miles—allow 2 and 4 hours

ROUTE—Bosley Locks—North Rode—Colleymill Bridge—Macclesfield Canal—Pool Bank—Timbersbrook—The Cloud—River Dane—Bosley Locks.

MAPS—O.S. 1:50,000 Sheet No 118—The Potteries
—O.S. 1:25,000 Pathfinder Series Sheet No SJ 86/96—Congleton.

CAR PARK—No official one.
—Layby—east of Locks on left of road.

ABOUT THE WALKS—The twelve Bosley locks are an impressive sight and looked down upon by the craggy face of The Cloud. This walk, slightly longer than most in this book, takes you past all the locks, over impressive aqueducts, past lakes and quiet lanes, and to the summit of The Cloud, an unsurpassed viewpoint over the Cheshire Plain. The shorter walk includes all the locks, and upon reaching the canal from North Rode you simply turn left along it to return to your starting point. The walk begins beside the A54 which cuts across the Bosley Locks; there is car parking space beside Station Road, just off the A54, and this is where I have begun the walk.

WALKING INSTRUCTIONS—Return to the A54 road and turn left and left again onto the towpath with the canal locks on your right. Keep beside the canal for ½ mile to Bridge No 54. Just after passing under it turn left to the road and turn right and follow it to the railway line, passing Station Road on your left. Just after where the road turns sharp right, continue ahead and, as footpath signed, walk along the drive of Manor House. After ¼ mile pass a lake on your right, and at the end of the woodland turn left to a stile and walk between the oak trees to North Rode, reached via a stile. Follow the farm road round eventually to your left to the church and village hall on your right. Turn left along Church Lane and after ¼ mile right at the path sign—Eaton. The pathline keeps the field boundary well to your right as you head for a stile. Over this bear left close to the field edge to a footbridge over the Cow Brook, and ascend to the road (A54) opposite Colley Mill. Turn right along the road and cross the River Dane. ¼ mile later reach the canal bridge No 61 gained on your left. At the canal side the shorter, 4 mile, route turns left, and just ahead is the half timbered Crossley Hall Farm on your right. Keep on the canal back to the A54 road.

Those on the longer route turn right under the bridge 61 and keep beside the canal for 2½ miles, passing the outskirts of Congleton and sign, Co-Op store ¼ mile. A mile later pass under bridge 70, then a railway bridge and leave the canal at the footbridge immediately afterwards. Cross to the other side into the trees on a track. Continue ahead into a large field and after ¼ mile gain the field boundary and bear right onto a track, which you follow straight ahead to the houses and minor road. Turn left and after 75 yards right onto the walled track of Acorn Lane. After ¼ mile

WALK 11—MOW COP—6 miles.

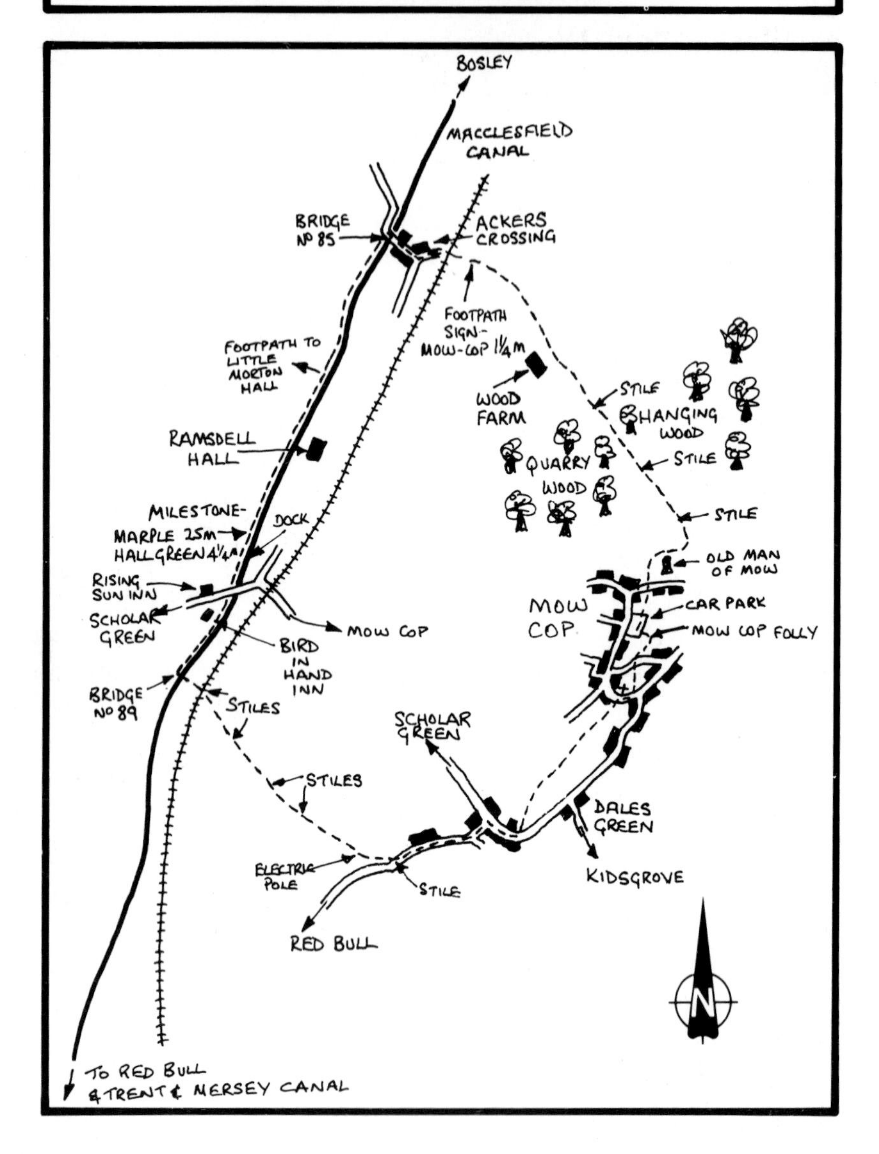

MOW COP—1,000 feet above sea level and a magnificent viewpoint over the Cheshire Plain stands the folly known as Mow Cop Castle, built in 1750 by Randle Wilbraham. The summit had a Beacon Tower and was used to signal the Spanish Armada, but has long since gone. Closeby is the rock pinnacle known as the Old Man of Mow Cop and both now belong to the National Trust. A stone beneath the "castle" records the site was used in 1807 for the first meeting of the Primitive Methodists. The Staffordshire Way (92 miles) and the Mow Cop Trail starts from here.

MACCLESFIELD CANAL—WALK NO 11

6 miles—allow 2½ miles

ROUTE—Mow Cop—Dales Green—Bridge No 89—Macclesfield Canal—Ackers Crossing—Roe Park—Hanging Wood—Old Man of Mow—Mow Cop.

MAPS—O.S. 1:50,000 Sheet No 118—The Potteries
—O.S. 1:25,000 Pathfinder Series Sheet No SJ 85/95—Kidsgrove and Leek.

CAR PARK—beneath Mow Cop.

ABOUT THE WALK—Dominating the skyline of the southern end of the Macclesfield Canal and adjoining Trent & Mersey Canal is Mow Cop folly. The view from here over the Cheshire Plain and beyond is extensive. Unlike the majority of the walks in this book you start the walk well away from the canal and descend to it. You walk beside it, northwards, for almost two miles passing the Bird in Hand Inn and the attractive Ramsdell Hall. At Ackers Crossing you ascend through particularly unspoilt woodland to regain Mow Cop and the pinnacle of the Old Man of Mow—National Trust property.

WALKING INSTRUCTIONS—The first part of the walk is the hardest to follow, not because the paths are not used but because of the complexity of the area. Basically you keep to the crest of the ridge as you descend and at all junctions keep ahead. From the car park beneath the folly, as guided by the path sign—The Cloud 6 miles—ascend the track to pass directly underneath the folly on your right. Follow the track/path around to your right and close to the houses left on the path which soon swings right. Keep on this track to Bellapois House. Here turn left then right immediately and continue on the track for 100 yards before turning left down a path and crossing a new road and housing estate to continue on the path to the next road. Turn right to pass the Hillside Methodist Chapel on your right. A little further turn left onto the track of Rockside Road. Now you begin descending, firstly past several houses before following the spine of the ridge, keeping ahead at all junctions; sometimes a path, sometimes a track. Continue past a quarry on your left before crossing a tarmaced path close to No 45 Rockside. Continue ahead soon to descend into a small rocky dale before gaining the houses of Dales Green. Turn right and follow the road round to your right and after 100 yards take the first road on your left. This is the end of the hard bit!

Continue descending down the road past the 30 mph sign and 200 yards later at the entrance drive to 86 The Hollow, on the left of the entrance is the stile and path. First you head for an electric pole before bearing right to a stile. Beyond is another stile and footbridge. Continue descending gradually to woodland and a stile. The path here is well defined as you walk through the woodland and after ¼ mile keep to the righthand path. This soon brings you into the open fields before passing under the railway line. Beyond you bear slightly left to gain Bridge No 89 and the canal. On the otherside of the bridge bear right and right shortly afterwards to reach the towpath.

Turn left and follow the path with the canal on your right. Keep on the canal for almost two miles, passing the Bird in Hand Inn and Ramsdell Hall on your right. At bridge No 85 leave the canal and turn right along the road over the canal into Ackers Crossing.

Follow the road to the righthand bend and turn left along the No Through Road. Cross the railway line and a few yards later gain the track beside the path sign—Mow Cop 1¼ miles. Ascend the track bearing right on it at the entrance to Wood Farm. A little further and as guided by signs leave the track to path gate and continue ascending up the field to walk well to the right of the house on your left. At the top lefthand corner of the field is the stile and well defined path. Follow this to your left then right as you continue ascending through woodland. At the end of the wood and near the end of the climb you reach a stile and emerge into open fields. Keep the field boundary on your right as you gently ascend and curve round to your right, passing through several stiles, heading for the pinnacle of the Old Man of Mow. Turn right at the track and shortly afterwards left to pass beneath the pinnacle. At the end of the path bear right then left on a path back to the car park beneath the folly. Again you can savour the view—this time you have earned it!

MOW COP

DANE AQUEDUCT, MACCLESFIELD CANAL

RAMSDEN HALL

WALK 12—SCHOLAR GREEN—10 miles.

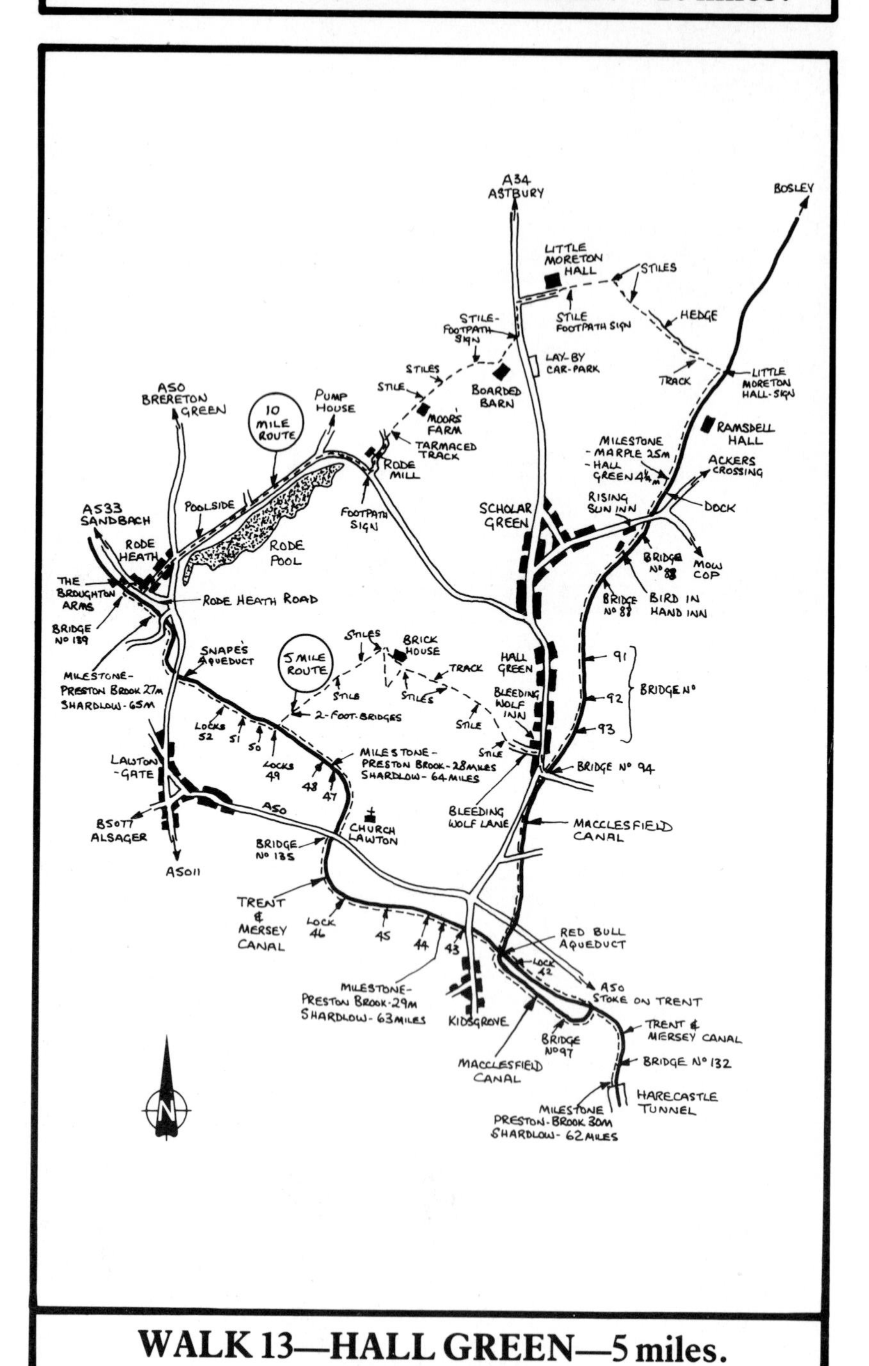

WALK 13—HALL GREEN—5 miles.

MACCLESFIELD CANAL AND TRENT & MERSEY CANAL—WALK NO 12

10 miles—allow 5 hours

ROUTE—Scholar Green—Macclesfield Canal—Little Morton Hall—Rode Mill—Rode Pool—Rode Heath—Trent & Mersey Canal—Macclesfield Canal—Harecastle Tunnel entrance—Trent & Mersey Canal—Macclesfield Canal—Scholar Green.

MAPS—O.S. 1:50,000 Sheet No 118—The Potteries
—O.S. 1:25,000 Pathfinder Series Sheet No SJ 85/95—Kidsgrove and Leek.

CAR PARK—No official one at Scholar Green.
National Trust car park at Little Morton Hall.

ABOUT THE WALK—One of the longest walks in the book BUT probably the finest canal circuit walk to be done. It is in many ways a grandslam of canal features, linking together the Macclesfield and Trent and Mersey canals, seeing locks, aqueducts, the famous Harecastle tunnel, a "two laned" canal (Trent and Mersey) and the "single" laned (Macclesfield) canal and passing the incredible Little Morton Hall. The folly of Mow Cop is always on the horizon, and numerous pubs along the way together with narrow boats passing through the locks, combine to make this a very memorable walk.

WALKING INSTRUCTIONS—Whilst the walk can be started from several locations, such as Red Bull and Rode Heath, I prefer to start from near the Rising Sun Inn, close to the Macclesfield Canal on the north eastern outskirts of Scholar Green. My reason is simply aesthetic, letting the walk unfold in wonder as you progress. Just up from the inn, gain the canal by the righthandside and at the canal left under the bridge. Shortly afterwards pass a canal dock on your right and canal milestone on your left—Marple 25 miles, Hall Green 4¼ miles. ¼ mile later pass the imposing Ramsdell Hall on your right, and a further ¼ mile brings you to a canal bridge and path signs for Little Morton Hall. Here, just before the bridge, leave the canal and turn left, guided by the stile and signs. The path soon joins a track before reaching a stile and path sign. Here you bear right, keeping the hedge on your right. After the second stile you bear left to a stile close to Little Morton Hall. Continue ahead past the Hall and along the drive to the A34 road.

LITTLE MORETON HALL—Dating from the 16th century it is a stunning moated manor house and one of the best examples of black and white design in the country. The property is now cared for by the National Trust and contains an exceptional cobbled courtyard, well tended gardens and numerous rooms rich in carvings, including the long gallery, 68 feet long by 12 feet wide.

Turn left along the main road for 150 yards to a stile and path sign on your right. Go through the stile and keep beside the hedge on your left to the next stile. Ascend the next field, keeping to the right of Boarded Barn Farm to a track, where bear right to gate, stile and footpath sign. The path line is well signed as you walk around the field edges to pass Moor's Farm. Here you walk along a tarmaced track, bearing left then right on it to pass Rode Mill and gain the minor road—Scholar Green/Rode Heath. Turn right and follow the road round to your left, with Rode Pool in the trees to your left. Keep on the road for almost a mile to the A50 road on the fringe of Rode Heath. Cross and walk along Chapel Lane. At the end gain the A533 road. Turn right along it past Rode Heath Post Office, and just afterwards left in front of The Broughton Arms and cross bridge No 139 over the Trent and Mersey Canal, where turn left onto the canal towpath. You keep on this for the next three miles, crossing Snape's Aqueduct and a whole string of locks—52 to 47—near Church Lawton. After passing under bridge 135 carrying the A50 road you pass another series of locks—46 to 43—before approaching Pool Aqueduct carrying the Macclesfield canal at Red Bull. Here ascend to the left to the Macclesfield Canal and turn right over the aqueduct, following the Macclesfield Canal to its junction with the Trent and Mersey Canal. Here ascend the bridge No 98 and keep right beside the Trent and Mersey Canal to follow it to the entrance of the Harecastle Tunnel, ½ mile away.

Retrace your steps back to bridge 98 and cross it to continue beside the Trent and Mersey Canal past the Bluebell Inn and lock 42. Regain Pool Lock Aqueduct and bear right following the Macclesfield Canal northwards for the next couple of miles back to Scholar Green. In walking order you pass under bridge 94—used on the shorter walk No 13—and further bridges to no 88 just after the Bird in Hand Inn. Just afterwards you approach your starting out path and bridge. Leave the canal here.

LITTLE MORETON HALL

MACCLESFIELD CANAL AND TRENT & MERSEY CANAL—WALK NO 13

5 miles—allow 2½ hours

ROUTE—Hall Green—Brick House—Bratt's Wood—Trent & Mersey Canal—Macclesfield Canal—Harecastle Tunnel entrance—Trent & Mersey Canal—Macclesfield Canal—Hall Green.

MAPS—O.S. 1:50,000 Sheet No 118—The Potteries
—O.S. 1:25,000 Pathfinder Series Sheet No SJ 85/95—Kidsgrove and Leek.

CAR PARK—No official one at Hall Green or on the route.

ABOUT THE WALK—A short walk linking the two canals together, illustrating the difference between a principal—Trent & Mersey Canal—with a lesser one—the Macclesfield Canal. You follow a section of each, see where they cross over and join, and see the famous Harecastle tunnel. Much of the walk is described on Walk No 12.

WALKING INSTRUCTIONS—The walk can be started from Red Bull, but for simplification of the link path in conjunction with Walk No 12 I have started it from Bridge No 94 on the Macclesfield Canal, close to Hall Green and the A34 road. From Bridge 94 ascend to minor road and turn left to the A34. Opposite to your right is the Bleeding Wolf Inn. Turn left in front of the thatched inn along Bleeding Wolf Lane. Bear right at the end keeping on a grass track, at the end of which is a stile. Keep the field boundary on your right as you cross the next field to a stile. The next field you cross in the middle, bearing left to the bottom lefthand corner to a stile and track which you follow to the track junction close to Brick House. Turn left along the track to the end of the field on your right. Turn right and cross the field to a stile in the righthand corner. Turn sharp left and follow the path beside Bratt's Wood on your right. It is well stiled. Descend to a stream and cross the footbridge before turning left across another and ascending the well defined path to the Trent & Mersey Canal, at Lock 49. Turn left and as detailed in Walk No 12 follow the canal towpath all the way to Harecastle Tunnel before following the Macclesfield Canal northwards to bridge No 94.

RED BULL AQUEDUCT

WALK 14—END TO END WALK—27¾ miles.

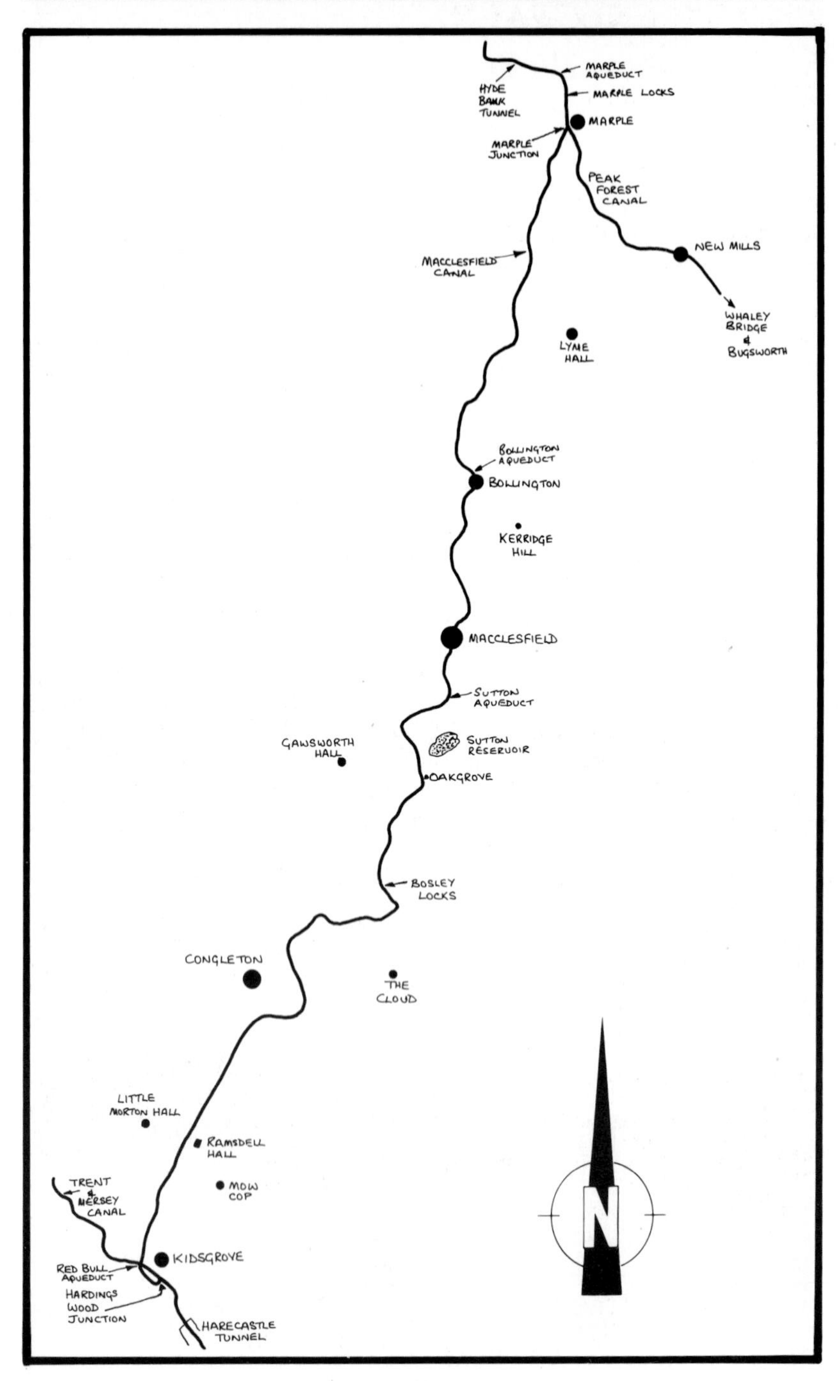

MACCLESFIELD CANAL—WALK NO 14 -

END TO END WALK

27¾ miles—10 to 12 hours of walking

MAPS—O.S. 1:50,000 Sheet No 118—The Potteries
—O.S. 1:50,000 Sheet No 109—Manchester

ABOUT THE WALK—Psychologically walking southwards is like walking downhill, and is for this reason why I prefer to start the end to end walk from the Marple Junction. There is no objection to starting from the Hardings Wood end; but heading northwards is "uphill"! Whilst it is possible and a hard walk to do the entire canal length in a day, the end to end concept does lend itself to a very enjoyable two day or weekend walk, stopping at an inn overnight on the way. At either end are the start of major populations and industry, leaving the vast majority of the route passing through unspolit scenery with the Peakland hills forming an attractive backcloth. The Bosley Locks are approximately half-way and are one of the canals finest features. Macclesfield or Congleton area make a good overnight halt.

JUNCTION OF THE TRENT & MERSEY AND MACCLESFIELD CANALS

TRENT & MERSEY CANAL FROM RED BULL AQUEDUCT

HARECASTLE TUNNEL—NORTHERN END

TRENT & MERSEY CANAL

First known as the Grand Trunk—was authorised on 14th May 1766 with a capital of £150,000. James Brindley surveyed the route—93⅜ miles from Derwent Mouth on the Trent to Preston Brook on the Bridgewater Canal near Runcorn. Work began immediately and by 1777 the whole canal was open with 76 locks.

The principal movers in the project were Erasmus Darwin and Josiah Wedgwood who saw it as a need for the Potteries and Midlands area. The major problem in construction was the 2,900 yard long Harecastle Tunnel. Many were sceptical that the canal company would ever pay a dividend but in 1781 5% was paid and in 1825 a £100 share was worth £2,300.

A separate book will be dealing with much of the canal in the Burton and Stafford area, but for the purposes of continuity, the section between the Macclesfield Canal junction and Caldon Canal junction is detailed in this book. The Shardlow area is covered in Volume One of this series. However, the Stoke on Trent section is particularly interesting having the remarkable Harecastle Tunnel.

Approaching the tunnel two tunnels can be seen. The original one built by James Brindley, took eleven years to construct, is now closed. The tunnel—9 feet wide and 1¾ miles long was an unprecidented undertaking in the late 18th century. There was no towpath and horses had to led over the hill while the boat was legged through. As a result there was considerable time loss while boats were moved through. In 1822 Thomas Telford suggested that another tunnel be constructed next to the existing one, and this was completed in 1827 with towpath. The two tunnels then operated on a one-way system greatly reducing the traffic conjestion. Mining subsidence gradually made Brindley's tunnel unusable and by 1918 had been abandoned. By the 1950's the other tunnel was suffering from subsidence and part of the towpath had to be removed. Between 1973-1977 the tunnel was closed for major repairs but is once again operational. Plaques on the southern entrance record the tunnel's history and a canal milepost that once stood on the horse path is now here. I have detailed a walk that links both ends of the tunnel.

TRENT & MERSEY CANAL WITH MOW COP IN THE DISTANCE

WALK 1—KIDSGROVE—5 miles.

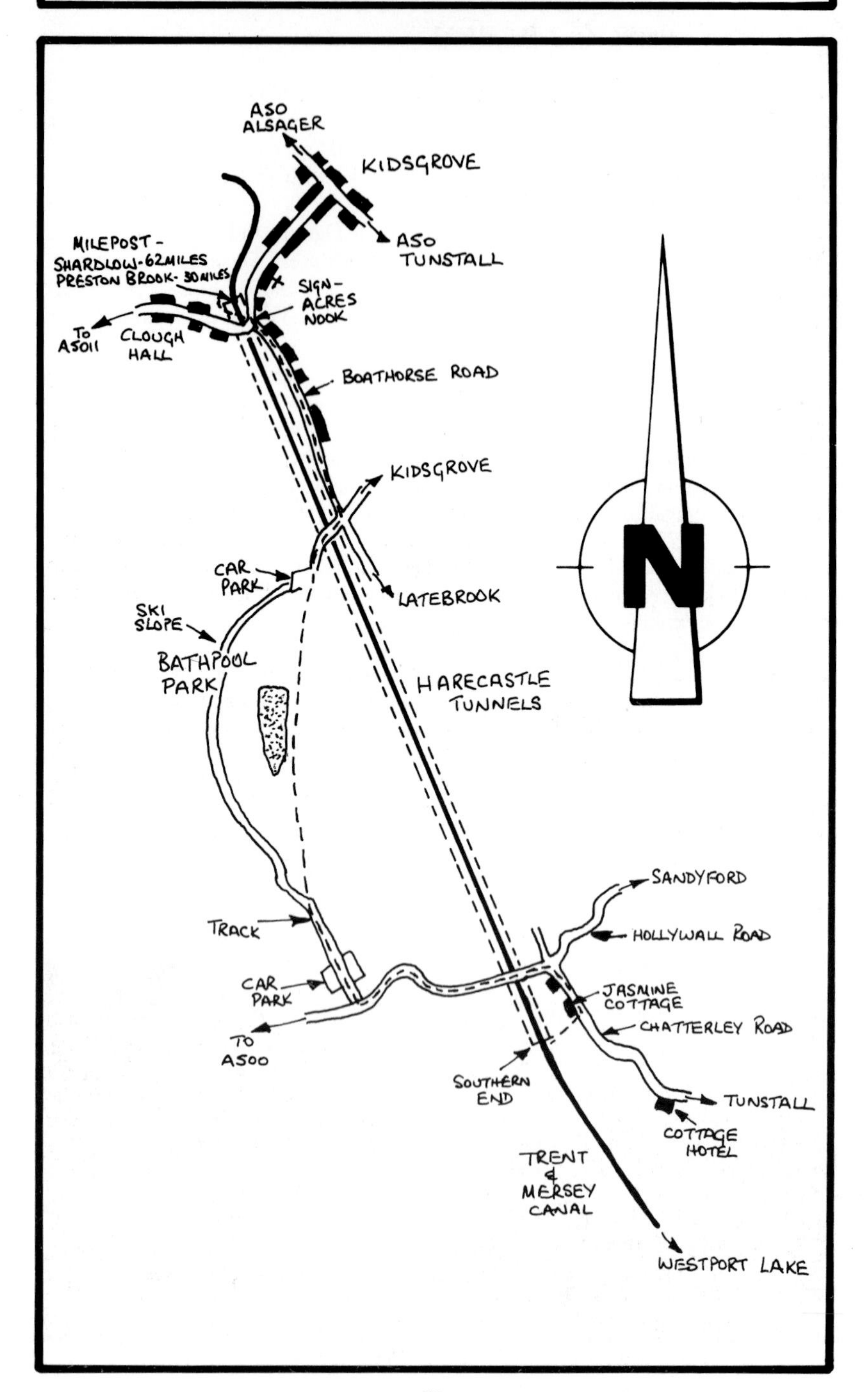

TRENT & MERSEY CANAL—WALK NO 1

5 miles—allow 2½ hours

ROUTE—Kidsgrove—northern end of Harecastle Tunnel—Bathpool Park—southern end of Harecastle Tunnel. Return same way.

MAPS—O.S. 1:50,000 Sheet No 118—The Potteries

CAR PARK—northern and southern end of Bathpool Park.

ABOUT THE WALK—The Harecastle Tunnel was one of the major canal undertakings in the 18th century. The orginal Brindley Tunnel is now closed and when in use the boats were legged through; the horses being led over the hill. The second tunnel originally had a towpath but is now mostly lost or submerged, due to subsidence. The original horse route has gone and the only way to join both ends of the 1¾ mile long tunnel by foot is via the Bathpool Park. Historically the walk is fascinating to see both ends of the tunnel and to watch the boats setting off on their subterranean journey. Car parking at either end is a problem but car parks in Bathpool Park bring you to within ½ mile of either end. A short return walk brings you to both ends.

WALKING INSTRUCTIONS—From the northern end of the tunnel ascend the walled track on your right which passes a memorial garden on your left before you descend to the road. Bear right along it and turn left along the signposted road—Acres Nook—along the aptly named road, Boathorse Road. After ½ mile gain a crossroads and turn right into Bathpool Park. The car park is on your right but keep to the lefthand path/track which passes woodland and later the lake on your right. After ½ mile the path reaches a track and turn left along this to the minor road and southern Bathpool Park car park.

Turn left along the road for ½ mile and turn right along Chatterley Road. Almost immediately bear right just after Jasmine Cottage and descend to the southern entrance of the Harecastle Tunnel. Return the same way.

SOUTHERN END OF HARECASTLE TUNNEL —BRINDLEY'S TUNNEL ON LEFT

CALDON CANAL NEAR HAZELHURST JUNCTION

LEEK TUNNEL

CALDON CANAL

Opened in 1779 as a branch of the Trent & Mersey Canal.

Length—17 miles from Etruria Junction to Froghall, with 17 locks.

The canal was owned by the Trent & Mersey Canal Company and built to transport the limestone from Caldon Low quarries. Much of the Froghall Basin buildings date from 1811. Limestone was brought here from the quarry via tramways and many of their routes can be traced today. In 1797 a branch was built to Leek from the Hazelhurst Junction near Denford, partly as a feeder for the canal using the recently built Rudyard Lake. The actual layout of the junction had to be altered in 1841 when the Leek railway was constructed. Today there is an impressive cross over with the Hazelhurst Aqueduct. The Leek branch can be followed to the fringe of the town and the restored 130 yard long Leek tunnel can be walked over. The canal ends as a stone aqueduct over the Churnet River.

In 1811 the canal was extended by 13 miles from Froghall to Uttoxeter. But, its use was shortlived with the construction of the railway in 1845—now also gone! The railway follows much of the line of the canal and sections can still be traced—see Walk No 1. In 1832 the rates of tonnage on the Caldon, Leek and Uttoxeter Canals was a penny per ton per mile. The cost from Etruria to Uttoxeter was 2 shillings and 6 pence (12½p). As with all canals the advent of the railway proved disastrous for the canals and trade rapidly declined. In fact the canal was owned by a railway company -the North Staffordshire Railway—and there was little point in competing with itself. By the beginning of this century it was little used and by 1960 hardly navigable. The Caldon Canal Society began the task of getting support to have it restored and in 1974 was opened again. Today it is one of the loveliest canals in Britain.

During the Summer at Froghall trips on a horse drawn narrowboat are available, with the operators wearing period costume and serving afternoon tea on board. The first part of the journey is exciting as you are legged through the Froghall Tunnel. At Consall Forge are the remains of industry and the Black Lion Inn, whose canalside setting is particularly attractive. Cheddleton has an operational flint mill while southwards is the Hollybush Inn at Denford, the Hazelhurst Aqueduct and junction. At Stockton Brook are several lochs and almost at Etruria are two staircase locks.

CANAL MILEPOST—CALDON CANAL

WALK 1—ALTON—5 miles .

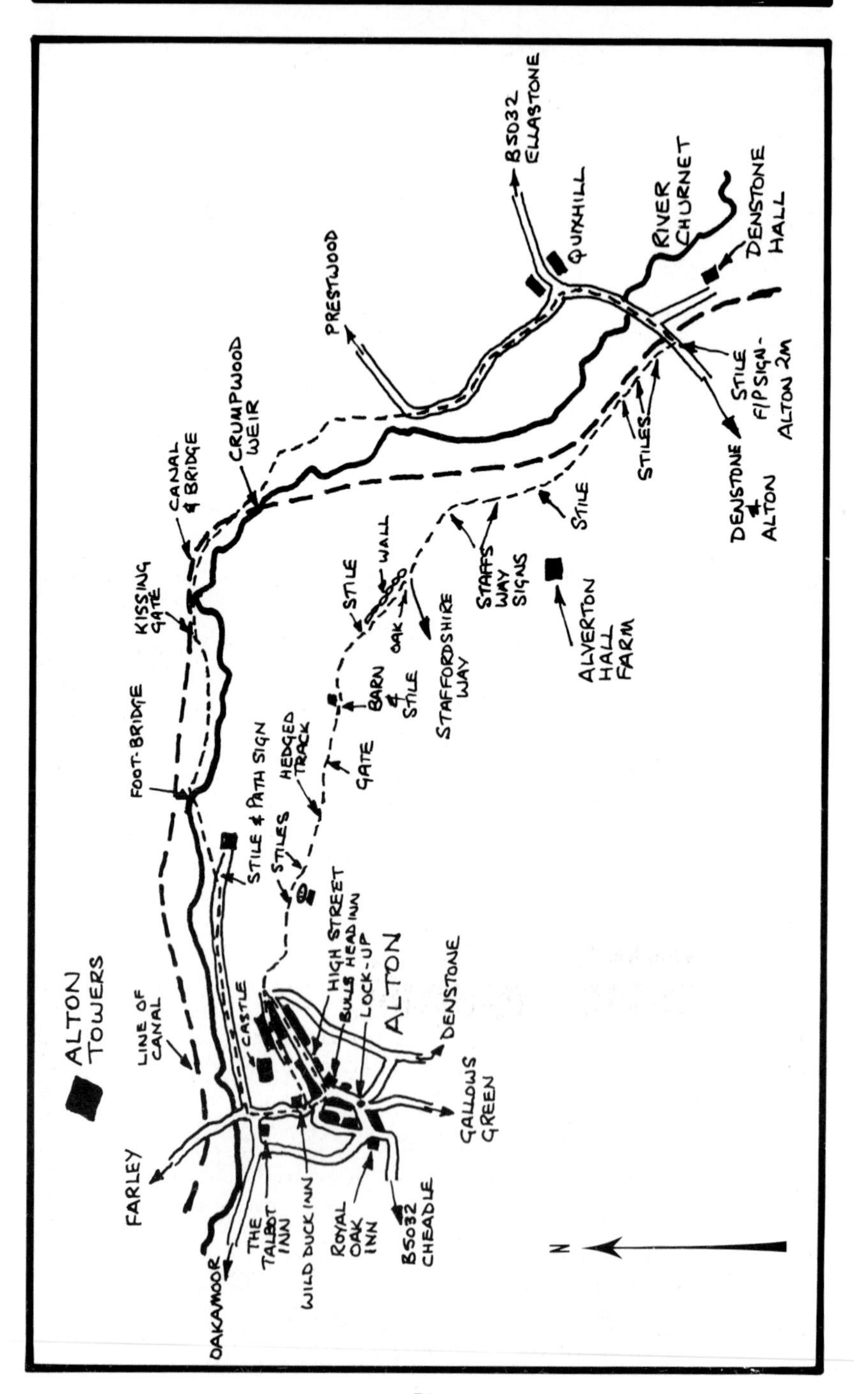

CALDON CANAL—WALK 1—5 MILES—Allow 2½ hours

ROUTE—Alton—River Churnet—Crumpwood Weir—Quixhill Lane—Quixhill—Denstone—Staffordshire Way—Town Head—Alton.

MAPS—O.S. 1:25,000 Sheet No. SK 04/14—Ashbourne and the Churnet Valley.

CAR PARK—No official one in Alton.

ABOUT THE WALK—Alton is a particularly attractive village and well worth exploring to see the Lock-Up, Church, High Street and impressive Castle. This walk encircles the village and valley, and follows a fragment of the now-abandoned Uttoxeter branch of the Caldon Canal. On the walk you can fully appreciate the magnificent setting of the Castle and valley.

WALKING INSTRUCTIONS— Starting from the High Street, descend the New Road northwards to the River Churnet, passing the Wild Duck Inn on your right. Just before the river and almost opposite the branch road on your left—Red Road and the Talbot Inn—turn right onto the track which runs underneath the Castle. For the next ½ mile keep on this through woodland and the river on your left. Nearing a private house pass through the stile on your left, as path signed, and continue ahead descending gently to the footbridge over the river. Cross the bridge and turn right, keeping to the middle of the field, with the river on your right and disused railway line on your left, for a little over ¼ mile. Pass a metal footbridge over the river before gaining a kissing gate on your left, and cross the railway line. You now walk beside the remains of the Canal to a splendid canal bridge, with the Crumpwood Switching Station close by. Here you join a tarmaced road and follow it to the impressive Crumpwood Weir. Keep on the road/track for another ¼ mile before turning right on the track to gain Quixhill Lane. Follow this for ½ mile to Quixhill.

CANAL BRIDGE NEAR DENSTONE

Turn right at the road, B5032, and follow it over the river and past Denstone Hall, well to your left. Just after the road turning on your left, continue over the railway bridge and as signposted—Alton 2 miles—leave the road and follow the well-defined path, now part of the Staffordshire Way. The path is well-stiled and signed as you keep to the righthand edge of the fields. After ¼ mile you begin to ascend with the remains of the canal below you on your right. Ahead can be seen Alverton Hall Farm, but follow the Staffordshire Way signs to the right of it and cross a large field to the field boundary on your left. Follow this round to a stile close to a large oak tree. After ascending the stile the Staffordshire Way continues to your left, but your route is to your right beside a wall on your right. Gain a stile on your right after 150 yards, and a further 100 yards brings you to a stone barn. The stile is on the other side of it. Continue ahead across the field before walking beside a hedge on your left to a gate. Here you reach a fenced track, which you follow for ½ mile to Alton, on the way passing a house and pond on your left. On reaching Alton, you can either keep ahead on Castle Hill, passing the Castle and descending Church Bank to the Wild Duck Inn, or bear left along Town Head and into the High Street.

BLACK LION INN, CONSALL FORGE

ALTON—The Churnet Valley at this point is dominated by the castellated towers of Alton Towers and Alton Castle and is known as the "Rhineland of Stafforshire." Alton Towers is now the home of the famous leisure park. The ruined buildings were built by Pugin for the 15th Earl of Shrewsbury. The grounds were landscaped by "Capability Brown." Alton Castle was also designed by Pugin and mostly dates from 1847 but includes part of the medieval building; it is now a Roman Catholic School. Alton is worth exploring for it has many interesting buildings including the famous round Lock Up, used to hold drunkards and prisoners early last century.

CALDON LOCK AT HAZELHURST JUNCTION

LEEK BRANCH (FROZEN) NEAR HORSE BRIDGE

WALK 2 & 3—FROGHALL—5 & 6 miles .

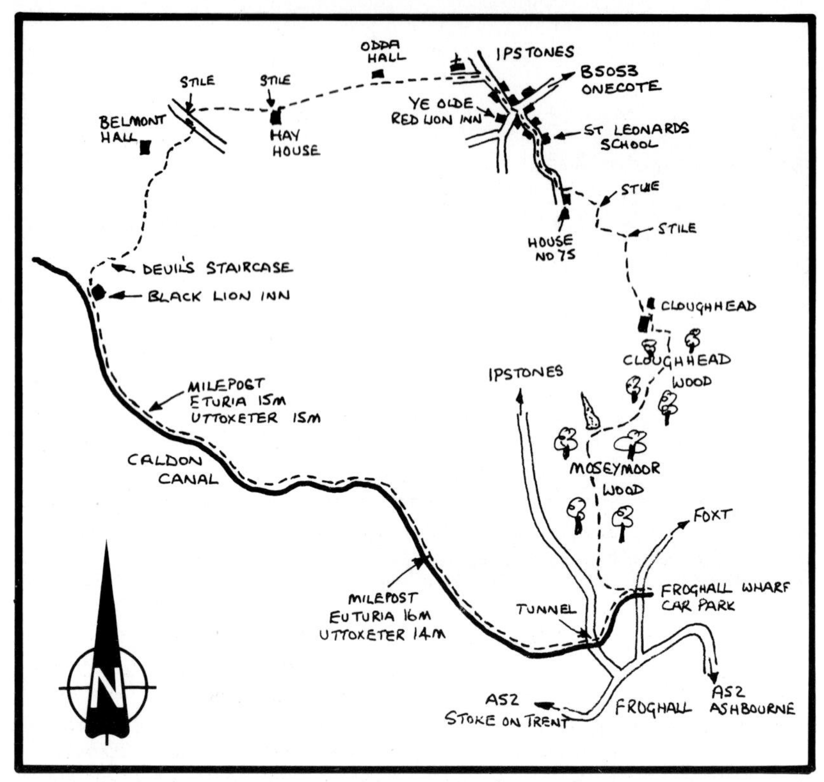

through the gate to the track, and just ahead on your left is the stile. Descend the field to the wood and bear right to the field's bottom righthand corner. The stile is not here, but ascend over the wall by the wooden barrier on your right and descend the path in the trees to the footbridge below. Do not cross the bridge but keep on the well-used path, first beside the stream then past a small lake on your right, before swinging left through Moseymoor Wood back to the Caldon Canal and your starting point.

CONSALL—OLD HALL

FROGHALL WHARF—The large copper works, moved from Oakamooor, remains. The limestone works around which the canal basin was built in 1811 has now gone but traces of its limekilns and tramways can still be seen. Trips on the canal on a horse drawn narrow boat, operate here during the summer months.

CALDON CANAL WALKS NOS 2 AND 3—5 & 6 MILES—Allow 2½ hours

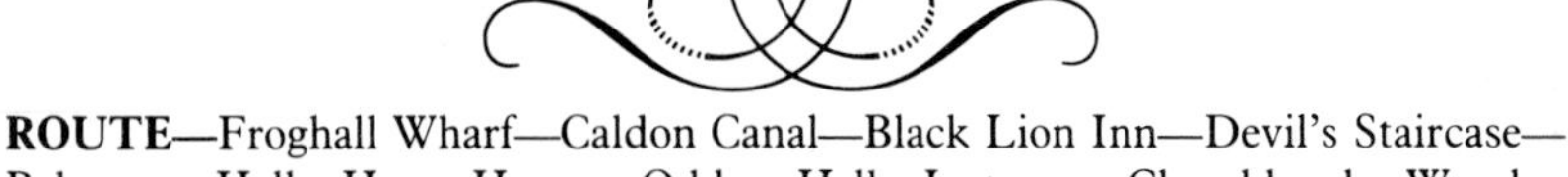

ROUTE—Froghall Wharf—Caldon Canal—Black Lion Inn—Devil's Staircase—Belmont Hall—Hay House—Odda Hall—Ipstones—Cloughhead Wood—Moseymoor Wood—Froghall Wharf.

MAPS—O.S. 1:50,000 Sheet No. 119—Buxton, Matlock and Dove Dale
—O.S. 1:25,000 Sheet No. SK 04/14—Ashbourne & The
Churnet Valley.

CAR PARK—Froghall Wharf.

ABOUT THE WALK—The walk offers two different types of walking, with the Caldon Canal as the central theme. The first walk of 5 miles is simply along the Canal to the Black Lion Inn at Consall Forge, whose remoteness and setting is quite unequalled. You return back along the Canal, after "walking for lunch". The longer walk of 6 miles ascends out of the valley to Ipstones before descending through very attractive woodland back to Froghall.

WALKING INSTRUCTIONS—From Froghall Wharf follow the Canal westwards to the tunnel, which you walk round, and continue beside the Canal for the next 2½ miles to the Black Lion Inn. Here the shorter walk retraces its steps beside the Canal back to Froghall. For the longer walk pass in front of the Inn and turn right on the path, which immediately bears left past the outbuildings and into woodland. The maps refers to the area as The Devil's Staircase, and you will certainly ascend hundreds of concrete steps to the top of the valley. The path is well used as you walk just inside the wood with a wall on your left, with Belmont Hall ahead. Upon reaching the Hall's drive, continue ahead along it for 40 yards to a stile and steps on your right. Turn right and descend and cross the footbridge and ascend to road beside path sign—"Consall Forge ¾ mile, Consall 2 miles". Turn left past Chapel House, and a few yards later right at the stile by the gate. This path is little used. First keep beside the field boundary for 30 yards before bearing right and ascending the field. Cross two fields and aim for the lefthand side of Hay House, where there is a stile. Cross to the next one on the right of the gate and continue across the field to another, keeping the wall on your right. Shortly afterwards you gain a walled track, passing Odda Hall on your left and trig. point—273 metres—on your right. Follow the track towards Ipstones, whose church tower has been a useful guideline.

Turn right along the road past the church and down to the B5053 road. Cross over into Brookfields Road, with the Old Red Lion Inn on the opposite side of the road. Descend the road past St. Leonards School and at House No. 75 turn left down beside it to a track and follow this past a barn on your right. Turn right just after, over a stile, and keep the field hedge on your left. Just before the end of the field turn left at the stile and keep the field boundary on your right to the next stile. Here turn right, now heading southwards, gently descending to Cloughhead Farm. Pass

WALK 4—CONSALL—6 miles .

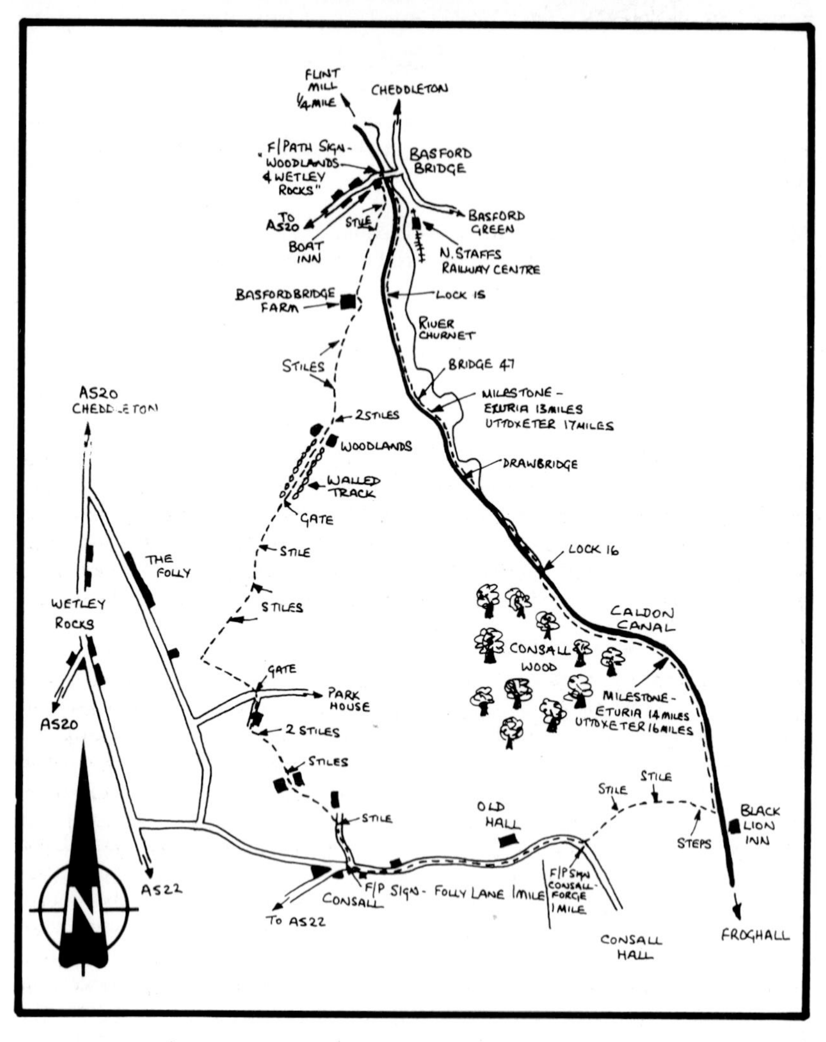

farm, whose track is reached via a stile. Go straight across with the farm buildings on your immediate right to a gate, keeping the field boundary on your left. Beyond you descend to a stile, passing another farm in the trees on your left. Over the stile gain the farm track and bear right up it to Consall and the path sign—Folly Lane 1 mile. Turn left and follow the road through Consall and past the Old Hall to your starting point.

CONSALL—The buildings of Consall Forge have almost gone but remains can still be found of this once busy point on the canal. Consall Old Hall dates from the 17th century and the New Hall was built in 1810.

CALDON CANAL—WALK NO 4

6 miles—allow 2½ hours

ROUTE—Consall—Consallforge—Caldon Canal—Basford Bridge—Woodlands—Consall.

MAPS:—0.S. 1:50,000 Sheet No 118—The Potteries
—O.S. 1:25,000 Pathfinder Series—Sheet No SJ 85/95—Kidsgrove and Leek.
—O.S. 1:25,000 Pathfinder Series—

CAR PARK—No official one but roadside parking near start of Consallforge footpath.

ABOUT THE WALK—The Consallforge area of the Caldon Canal is amongst the finest and remotest canal scenery in the Midlands. This walk encompass the area's remoteness, with the idyllically-situated Black Lion Inn and the Boat Inn at Basford Bridge. For your return to Consall you cross fields and follow tracks past farms before passing the magnificent Old Hall at Consall. The views from the fields of the Consall Wood and Churnet Valley are of the highest order. The paths are little used, but basically all the stiles and gates are there.

WALKING INSTRUCTIONS—From the eastern edge of Consall, leave the road at the path sign—Consallforge 1 mile. The path is defined as you basically descend, gradually at first before steeply down the many steps to the canal at Consallforge. To your right is the Black Lion Inn. Turn left and follow the towpath with the canal on your right to Lock 16. Here cross over and keep the canal on your left and for a while the River Churnet on your immediate right. 1½ miles later reach Basford Bridge and the Boat Inn. Ascend to the road, cross the bridge and turn left, as path signed—The Woodlands and Wetley Rocks—and walk past the inn to a stile. Much of the time you follow a track with the field boundary on your left to Basfordbridge Farm. Here bear left beneath it beside the field boundary to a stile and brook. Keep on the track ahead, ignoring all side routes as you ascend the bends to a metal stile on the left of the gate. The path ahead is illdefined but simply keep the field boundary on your right as you ascend to the next stile. Two more are ahead as you approach The Woodlands.

Don't bear right on the walled track; instead keep ahead to a stile and continue through two more past the buildings to a walled track. Follow this for ¼ mile to its end and continue with the boundary on your left to the next stile and stream. Still keep the boundary on your left as you ascend gently to two more stiles. Ahead and to your right can be seen the houses on Folly Road. When almost opposite the top solitary one—the road is at the end of the field—turn left through the gate and keep beside the field boundary on your left to the gate and farm road. Continue ahead along the farm drive past the farm and curve round to your left to two stiles in the righthand corner of the field. Over this continue to a gate and on towards the next

WALKS 5,6,7,& 8—DEEP HAYES—2, 2½, 4½, & 7 miles.

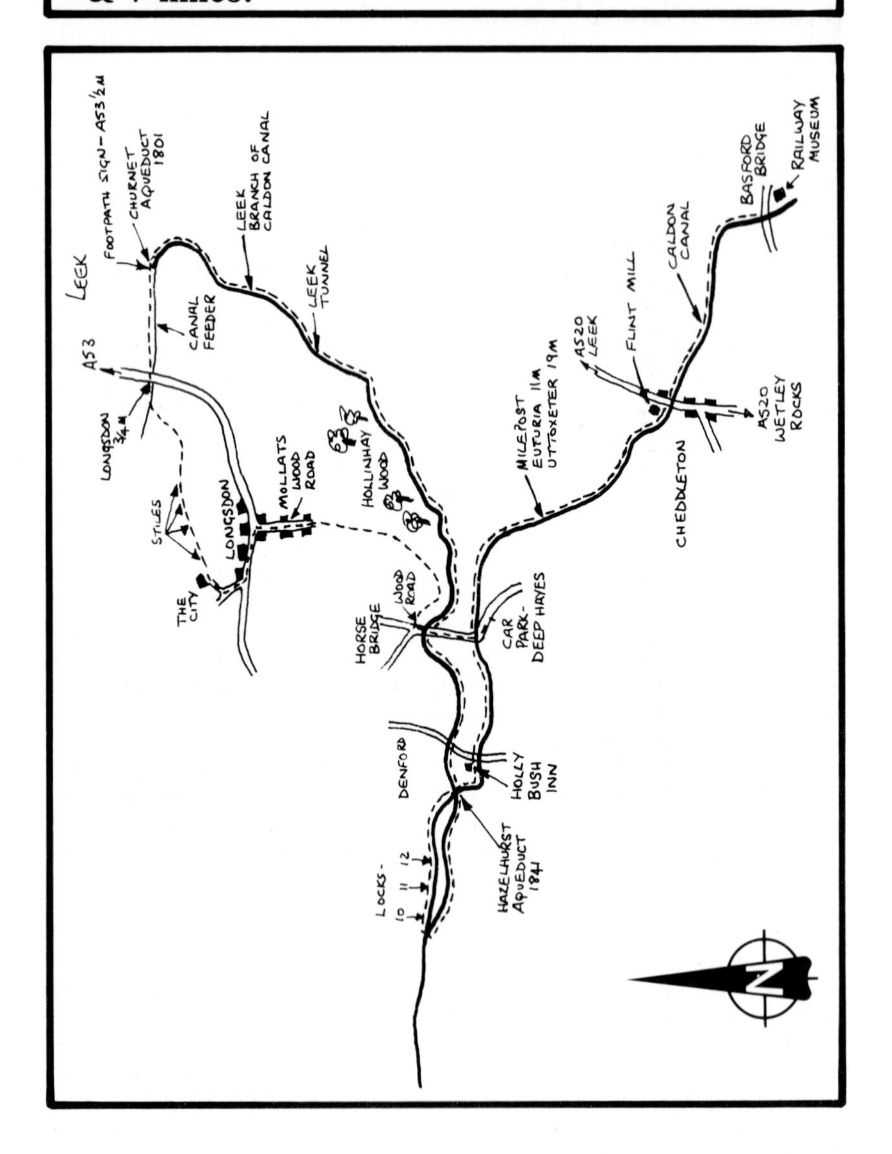

CHEDDLETON—The church on the hill, dedicated to St Edward the Confessor dates from the 12th century. Closeby are the village stocks and pinfold. The flint mill complete with two water wheels has been painstakingly restored and is open every weekend—sometimes a running demonstration is held. The former railway station is now a museum and headquaters of the North Staffordshire Railway Company. Train trips operate during the summer.

CALDON CANAL WALKS NOS 5, 6, 7, AND 8—2, 2½, 4½ and 7 miles - Allow 1 to 3 hours.

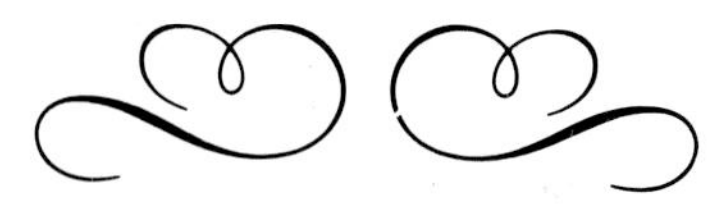

MAPS—O.S. 1:50,000 Sheet No. 118—The Potteries.
O.S. 1:25,000 Outdoor Leisure Map—The White Peak
(West Sheet)

CAR PARK—Deep Hayes—Grid Ref. SJ963534—opposite Horse Bridge.

ABOUT THE WALK—The Caldon Canal is a fascinating place to explore, and particularly so through such a picturesque area. There are several walk options described here of varying lengths, and all hinge on the Canal. Firstly there is the Froghall branch to Cheddleton and its amazing Flint Mill. Secondly there is the Leek branch, which uses a section of The Staffordshire Way for your return. Being a figure of eight, there are three walk options.

WALKING INSTRUCTIONS —

WALK 1—2 miles—From the car park descend to the Canal and turn right along it to Cheddleton to see its Flint Mill. Return the same way. The walk can be extended to continue along the Canal to Basford Bridge and Boat Inn, ½ mile away, to visit the Cheddleton Railway Museum.

WALK 2—2½ miles—From the car park descend to the Canal and turn left along it past the Holly Bush Inn at Denford, and under Denford Aqueduct to Lock 10 and the junction of the Leek branch. Cross over the metal bridge and follow the Leek branch for a little over a mile to Horse Bridge. Here leave the Canal and follow the road to your right over the Froghall branch back to the Car Park.

BOAT INN, BASFORD BRIDGE, CALDON CANAL

WALK 3—4½ miles—From the car park descend to the Canal and follow the road to Horse Bridge. Turn right and follow the Leek branch of the Caldon Canal for a little over 2 miles. First pass through Hollinhay Wood before reaching the Leek Tunnel, re-opened on April 3rd 1985. A path ascends over the hillside and rejoins the Canal, which you follow to the outskirts of Leek at the Churnet Aqueduct. Turn left as path-signed—A53 ½ mile. Basically you follow the canal feeder to the road. At the road you join The Staffordshire Way, waymarked with Staffordshire Knots. Cross the road as signed—Longsdon ¾ mile—and after 20 yards just after a stile turn left and follow the curving path beside the field boundary on your left. Gradually ascend to a stile and enter Longsdon Wood. Continue through it on a well-stiled path to the house known as The City, walking round its lefthand edge. Keep left at all road junctions to reach the A53 road. Turn left along the road, and about 130 yards later turn right into Mollats Wood Road. Keep straight ahead at all junctions and pass the houses as the road deteriorates into a track as you descend past bracken and woodland. Upon reaching a road (Wood Road), follow it round to your right past the houses to the minor road in Horse Bridge. Turn left along Sutherland Road and cross over the Canal and retrace your steps back to the Car Park.

WALK 4—7 miles. This is Walks 2 and 3 joined together.

LEEK—James Brindley, the canal engineer born near Wormhill, Buxton in Derbyshire, worked as a millwright here, before being "discovered" by the Duke of Bridgewater. Brindley died here in 1772 from an illness said to have contracted while surveying the Leek to Froghall canal. His mill and museum is open to the public in Mill Street. Last century silk mills were the main industry and although gone today there are still links with the past, with man made fibres being made and Europe's largest dye works. Surrounding the town, which has a population of 20,000, is the Staffordshire Moorlands area of the Peak Disirct National Park, with the rocks of the Roaches being particularly predominant.

CALDON CANAL AND HAZELHURST JUNCTION

CHEDDLETON FLINT MILL

WALKS 9, 10 & 11—ENDON BANK—4 & 6 miles

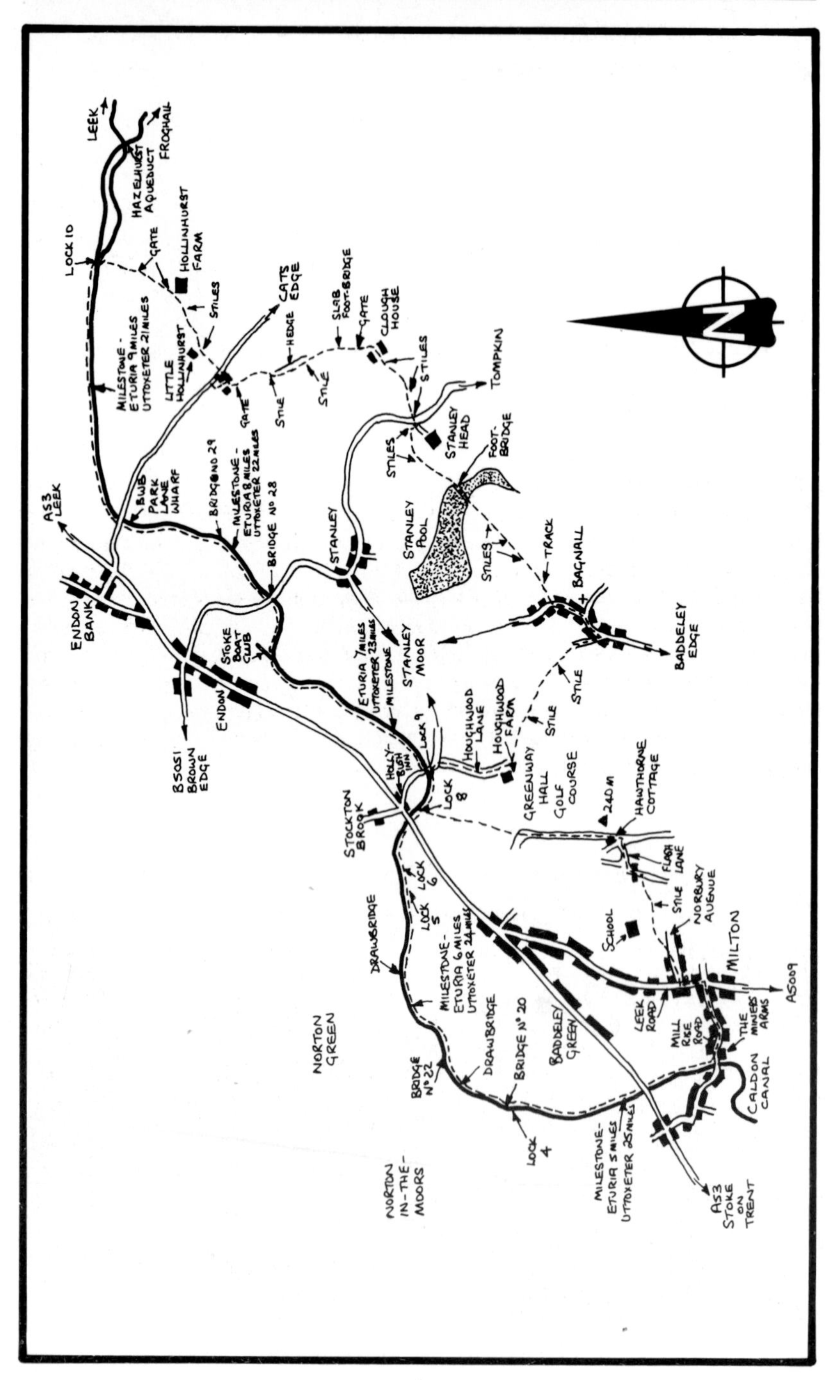

CALDON CANAL—WALK NOS 9, 10, & 11

10 miles together; individually—4 and 6 miles—allow 2, 3, and 4 hours.

ROUTE—Endon Bank—Caldon Canal to Leek branch—Hollinhurst Farm—Clough House—Stanley Head—Stanley Pool—Bagnall—Houghwood Farm—Caldon Canal—Milton—Baddeley Edge—Caldon Canal—Endon Bank.

MAPS—O.S. 1:50,000—Sheet No 118—The Potteries
—O.S. 1:25,000 Pathfinder Series—Sheet No SJ85/95—Kidsgrove and Leek.

CAR PARK—no official one

ABOUT THE WALK—a major exploration of the Caldon Canal from its junction with the Leek Branch in the north to Milton and the fringes of Stoke on Trent in the south. Usually I do the walk as a whole in the form of a figure of eight which enables the route to be either done in its entirety or as two individual walks of 4 and 6 miles long using Lock 8 near Stockton Brook as the hinge point. The northern longer part follows paths across the fields which in some cases are little used but all the stiles are there. The route crosses Stanley Pool and descends the edge of Stanley Moor back to the canal. The shorter southern route uses Baddeley Edge for the descent to the canal, providing stunning views of the canal. Doing the figure of eight route, the canal walking is broken up into sections, as you explore the surrounding countryside, providing much variety to the walk.

LOCKS, STOCKTON BROOK, CALDON CANAL

WALKING INSTRUCTIONS—The walk begins just east of Endon Bank where the Cats Edge road crosses the canal at the British Waterways Board, Park Lane Wharf. Follow the canal virtually due east for a mile to Lock 10 to the junction of the Leek Branch. Cross the metal bridge, dated 1842, and after passing under the next bridge turn left over it and leave the canal. Ascend the field to a gate in the top righthand corner. Continue ahead bearing right to a gate close to the buildings of Hollinhurst Farm. Cross the field to a stile beside an oak tree. At the other side of the next field pass over a stone gap and ahead can be seen the stile by a holly tree. A further stile can be seen with Little Hollinhurst on the right. Continue ahead past the house on your right to the field corner beside the road and farm drive. Turn right and left 30 yards later walking up the farm road, and in the main building block turn left to the gate. You follow a track bearing right in the second field to a stile. Through this turn right then left almost immediately keeping the field hedge on your left. This will bring you to a stile and a little later to a stile and slab footbridge. Over this bear right to a gate and follow the track to Clough House just ahead.

Turn right along the farm drive past the house to the end of the buildings. Don't use the stile ahead but the one on your left. Continue up the middle of the field and over the brow reach the next stile. Cross the next field with the stile being in the farn righthand corner. Ahead is Stanley Head. Turn left to the entrance gate and immediately right through the stile to the next one and turn left. You are now on a defined path as you descend the field to a stile. Keep ahead—not right—and follow the path along the edge of the trees of Stanley Head to gain the footbridge over Stanley Pool. At the end pass through a stile and ascend the field to another. The path is well stiled as you approach Bagnall, bearing right at the top along a track to the road. Turn left along it passing the church high on your left and following the road round to your right. Just past the village hall on your right turn right down the road/track; it is well gated. At the end of the track ascend the stile and bear left and keep to the high ground to reach the next stile as you follow a good path through moorland and descend to the Houghwood Lane beneath the farm. Turn right and descend the lane; at the bottom turn right, passing the Greenway Hall Golf Clubhouse on your left, and reach the canal at Lock 9. Here you can turn right and join the towpath and follow it back to your start near Endon Bank, 2 miles away.

Those on the complete circuit or 4 mile one, turn left onto the canal towpath and keep on it for the next 2 miles as it loops round to Milton. En route passing locks, drawbridges, and canal mileposts. After Milepost—Eturia 5 miles, Uttoxeter 25 miles—pass under the A53 road and just before the next bridge turn left to Mill Rise Road. Bear left along it through Milton to A5009 road junction and turn left along Leek Road. Take the second road on your right—Norbury Avenue—and after 50 yards bear left on the path which crosses estate roads before becoming a fenced path with a school on your left. Continue ascending up a field to another stile and follow the path to your left then right past the houses to a road. Turn right then left along a narrow lane, and where it levels out turn right along Flash Lane. At the end of this turn right then left almost immediately passing Hawthorne Cottage on your left. You are now on the crest of the ridge and keep on the lane past houses on your left and golf course on your right as you begin to descend. Where the road turns left, keep ahead on a well used path keeping to the high ground. Eventually you will regain the canal at Lock 8. Turn right to Lock 9 where the short 4 mile route ends. Those on the 10 mile route continue on the towpath, now on the lefthand side of the canal as you head northwards past further milestones, the Stoke Boat Club and on to Park Lane Wharf, and the road from Endon Bank, where you began.

BALANCING BRIDGE—CALDON CANAL

ETRURIA STAIRCASE LOCKS

WALK 12—HANLEY PARK—3 miles.

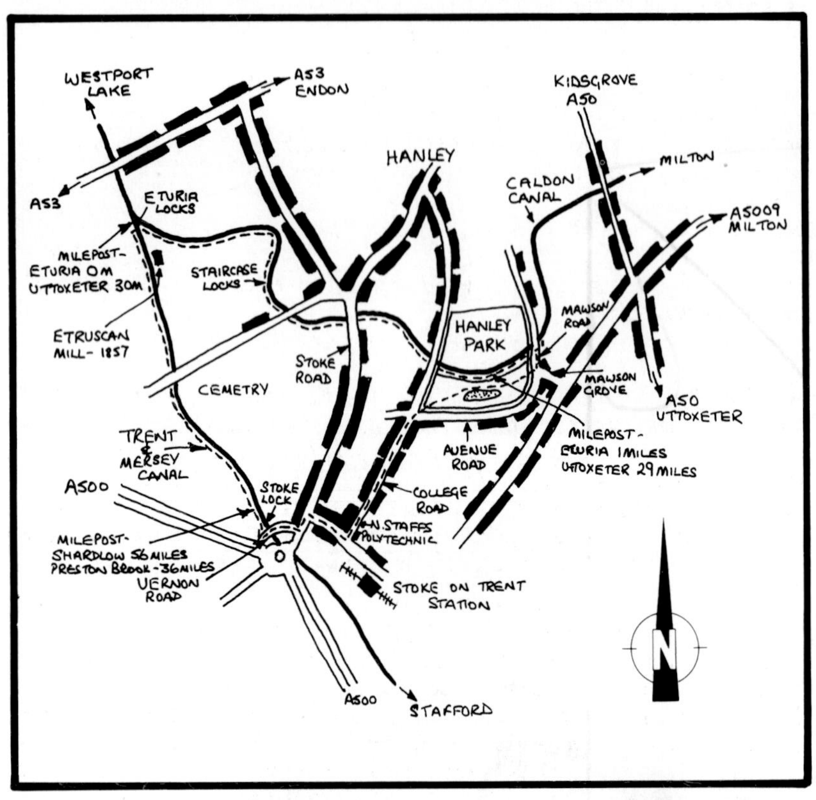

ETRUSCAN MILL, ETRURIA

CALDON CANAL—WALK NO 12

3 miles—allow 1½ hours

ROUTE—Hanley Park—Caldon Canal—Eturia Locks and junction with Trent & Mersey Canal—Trent & Mersey Canal—Hanley Park.

MAPS—O.S. 1:50,000 Sheet No 118—The Potteries

CAR PARK—no official one—roadside parking on Avenue and Ridgeway Road beside Hanley Park.

ABOUT THE WALK—The walk begins on the eastern edge of Hanley Park, where the canal is accessible—it is not from inside the park. The route follows the canal through Hanley and is particularly attractive with numerous bends and several locks, including two staircase locks. The junction with the Trent & Mersey is particularly important, complete with zero canal milepost. You now follow the Trent & Mersey Canal for a short distance before walking along roads to Hanley Park and your start. A delightful circular walk in the centre of the Potteries!

WALKING INSTRUCTIONS—Where Mawson Road beside Hanley Park crosses the canal, turn right down to the canal and turn left, passing under the Mawson Road bridge. Keep beside the canal on your right for a little over a mile to the Eturia Junction of the Trent & Mersey. Cross over and turn left along the Trent & Mersey Canal—on your left with the Etruscan Stone & Flint Mill. Pass the milepost—Shardlow 56 miles/Preston Brook 36 miles and at Stoke Lock just afterwards bear right to the road and turn left along Vernon Road. Turn left under the railway bridge and right into Station Road. Take the first road on your left—College Road—passing North Staffordshire Polytechnic. Follow this to the Avenue Road and entrance to Hanley Park. Bear right through the park passing the lake on your right and eventually gain Mawson Road. A little to your left is the canal where you began.

CALDON CANAL AT ETRURIA

WALK 13—MILTON—8 miles.

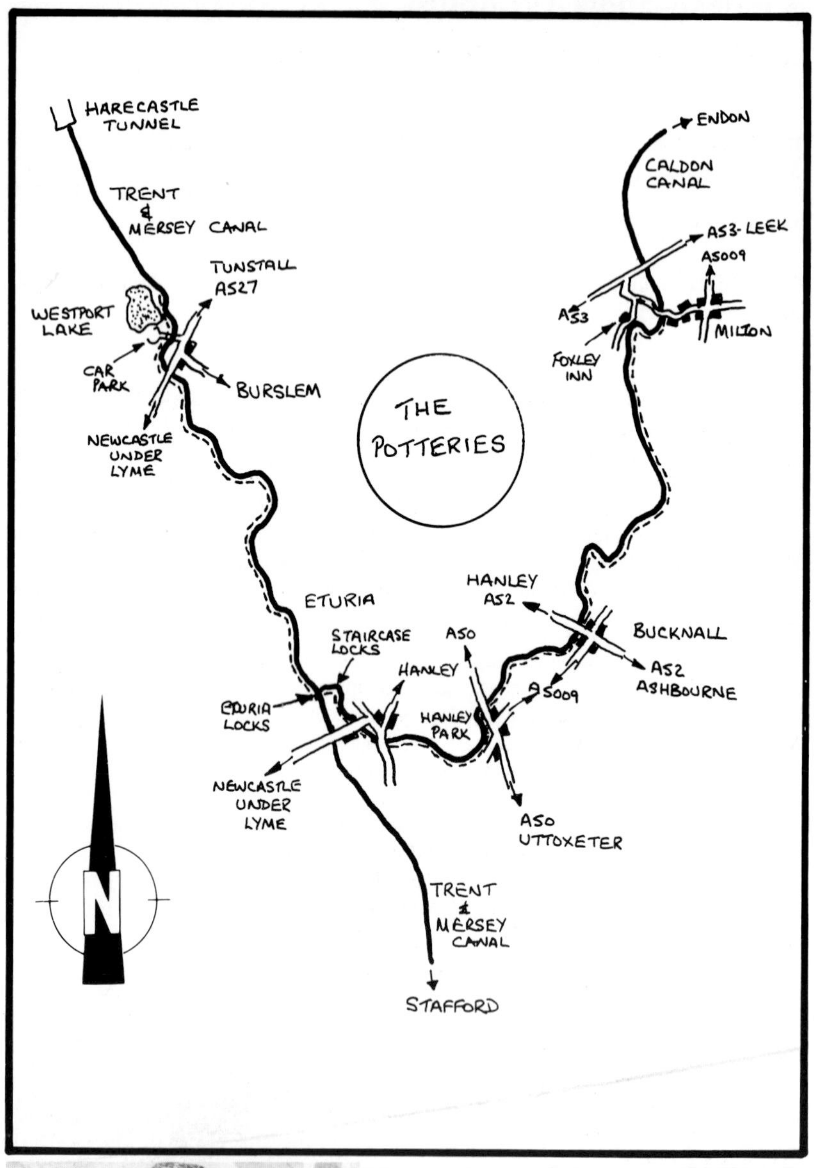

CANAL MILEPOST AT JUNCTION OF CALDON AND TRENT & MERSEY CANALS

CALDON CANAL AND TRENT & MERSEY CANAL—WALK NO 13

8 miles one way—allow 3 to 4 hours

ROUTE—Foxley Inn, Milton—Caldon Canal to Eturia Junction with the Trent & Mersey Canal—Trent & Mersey Canal—Westport Lake, Tunstall.

MAPS—O.S. 1:50,000 Sheet No 118—The Potteries

CAR PARK—Westport Lake, Tunstall

ABOUT THE WALK—a magnificent U-shaped walk through the heart of Stoke on Trent, passing numerous inns, locks, marinas, industrial architecture and unusual vantage points of the city. The canals are a haven in such a metropolis and for this reason I have made it a one way walk—there is nothing to stop you returning the same way making a level 16 mile walk. First you follow the Caldon Canal to its junction with the Trent and Mersey Canal. Here you head northwards beside it to Westport Lake. A further mile from here is the southern entrance of the Harecastle Tunnel. Whichever end you start from you can be assured of a really enjoyable outing.

WALKING INSTRUCTIONS—I prefer to start the walk at the canal bridge near the Foxley Inn in Milton. Here you are surrounded by fields as you head southwards along the Caldon Canal to Northwood, Bucknall and Hanley with its locks. At Eturia Junction turn right along the Trent & Mersey Canal and follow it northwards to Westport Lake more than 3 miles away.

THE FOXLEY INN, CALDON CANAL

WALKS 14, 15 & 16—END TO END WALKS–17 miles .

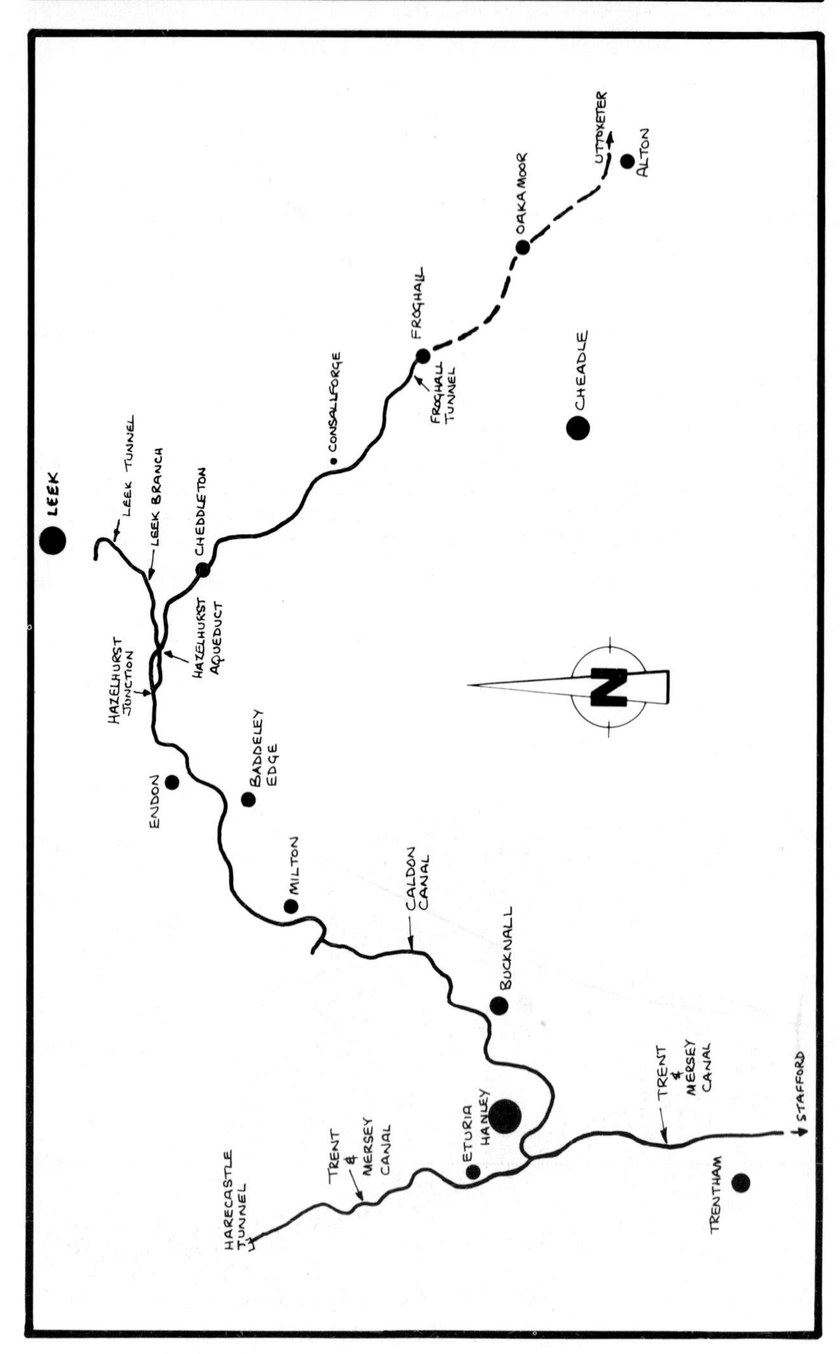

CALDON CANAL—WALK NO 14, 15, & 16

— END TO END WALK

Longest walk—17 miles—allow 6/7 hours

MAPS—O.S. 1:50,000 Sheet No 119 -Buxton, Matlock and Dovedale
—O.S. 1:50,000 Sheet No 118—The Potteries

ABOUT THE WALKS—Because of the Leek branch there are three permutations to walking the canal from end to end.

1. Froghall to Etruria—17 miles
2. Leek to Etruria—13 miles
3. Leek to Froghall—11 miles

All three explore the unique character of the canal and pass its major attractions such as the Hazelhurst Junction and nearby aqueduct; the remote Black Lion Inn; and Cheddleton Flint Mill. Walking end to end gives you at one fell swoop the unique flavour of the canal and cannot be stressed to fully what an enjoyable walk it is.

HAZELHURST JUNCTION, CALDON CANAL

CANAL FEATURES—to look for

STOP PLANKS—in various places can be seen vertical grooves in the canal wall with handled planks stacked nearby. The planks are slotted into the grroves sealing the canal while repairs or cleaning of drained section is carried out.

ROPE GROOVES— on the side of bridges, sometimes with cast iron shields, can be seen the grooves cut by the horse tow lines over the decades, such as the photograph below on the Peak Forest canal.

TURNOVER/CROSSOVER BRIDGES— in a few places the towpath switches sides of the canal and a bridge was built to enable the horse to cross over without unhitching the line. The Macclesfield canal has some excellent examples and near the junction with the Peak Forest canal is a horse tunnel.

SWING BRIDGES— as the name implies the bridge could be swung out of the way to allow boats to pass. Examples can be seen on the Peak Forest and Macclesfield canals.

BALANCED BRIDGES— bridges finely balanced that can be either pushed upwards out of the way or lowered across the canal. Exampes can be seen on the Peak Forest and Caldon canals.

SKEW BRIDGES— most canal bridges are built at right angles to the canal. In a few cases to avoid the Z bend in the road the bridge was built at an angle.

ROPE GROOVES, PEAK FOREST CANAL

CANAL MUSEUMS

1. The National Waterways Museum,
   The Boat Museum,
   Dockyard Road,
   Ellesmere Port,
   South Wirral.
   L65 4EF Tel. No 051-355 5017

2. British Waterways Board,
   Waterways Museum,
   Stoke Bruerne,
   Towcester,
   Northants.

OTHERS OF RELATED INTEREST —

1. **Paradise Mill,**
   Park Lane,
   Macclesfield.
   Cheshire. Tel No 0625-618228

2. **Silk Museum,**
   The Macclesfield Heritage Centre,
   Roe Street,
   Macclesfield.
   Cheshire. Tel No. 0625-613210

3. **Brindley Mill and Museum,**
   Mill Street,
   Leek.
   Staffordshire

4. **Cheddleton Flint Mill,**
   Cheddleton,
   Staffordshire

HARECASTLE TUNNEL—SOUTHERN ENTRANCE

CANAL SOCIETIES & USEFUL ADDRESSES

British Waterways Board,
Information Centre,
Melbury House,
Melbury Terrace,
London.
NW1 6JX

Northwich Area Engineer,
Navigation Road,
Northwich,
Cheshire.

Huddersfield Canal Society,
R.A. Dewey,
3 Pump Row,
Penistone Road,
High Flatts,
Huddersfield.
HD8 8XU

Macclesfield Canal Society,
c/o Endon Drive,
Brown Lees,
Biddulph,
Stafforshire.

Peak Forest Canal Society,
B.P. Stockdale,
34 Hulme Hall Avenue,
Cheadle Hulme,
Cheshire.

Trent & Mersey Canal Society,
M. D. Gray,
7, Cloverdale,
Weeping Cross,
Stafford.
ST17 4QJ

Caldon Canal Society,
H. V. Turner,
Broad Street Post Office,
Hanley,
Stoke on Trent,
Staffs
ST1 4JH

SUGGESTED FURTHER READING — a random selection

The Canals of the East Midlands Charles Hadfield David & Charles
The Canals of the West Midlands Charles Hadfield David & Charles
British Canals—an Illustrated History Charles Hadfield David & Charles 1979
James Brindley H. Bode Shire Publictions 1973
The Trent & Mersey Canal Lindsay David & Charles 1979
Nicholson/Ordnance Survey Guide to the Waterways—Vol 2—Central
Nicholson/Ordnance Survey Guide to the Waterways—Vol 3—North
Cheshire Ring Canal Walk—Vols 1,2,3 & 11—Cheshire County Council publications.
Canal Companion Cheshire Ring J.M.Pearson 1986
Discovering Canals in Britain Peter L.Smith Shire Publications 1981
Discovering Lost Canals Ronald Russell Shire Publications

OTHER CANAL WALK BOOKS BY JOHN N. MERRILL

Vol 1—Derbyshire and Nottinghamshire.
— more than 30 walks on the Chesterfield, Cromford, Erewash, Nutbrook, Derby, Nottingham and Trent & Mersey Canals.

Vol 3—Staffordshire
—30 walks on the Trent & Mersey canal.

FORTHCOMING —

Vol 4—The Cheshire Ring
—walk guide in stages to the 97 mile walk around the ring on the Macclesfield, Peak Forest, Ashton, Rochdale, Bridgewater, Trent & Mersey and Leeds & Liverpool canals.

Vol 5—Nottinghamshire, Leicestershire and Lincolnshire.
—deals with River Trent, Grantham Canal, River Soar, Witham Navigation, and Foss Dyke Navigation.

Vol 6—South Yorkshire.
—Barnsley Canal, River Don and Navigation, Staniforth and Keadby canal.

OTHER BOOKS BY JOHN N. MERRILL PUBLISHED BY JNM PUBLICATIONS

DAY WALK GUIDES -

SHORT CIRCULAR WALKS IN THE PEAK DISTRICT
LONG CIRCULAR WALKS IN THE PEAK DISTRICT
CIRCULAR WALKS IN WESTERN PEAKLAND
SHORT CIRCULAR WALKS IN THE STAFFORDSHIRE MOORLANDS
SHORT CIRCULAR WALKS AROUND THE TOWNS AND VILLAGES OF THE PEAK DISTRICT
SHORT CIRCULAR WALKS AROUND MATLOCK
SHORT CIRCULAR WALKS IN THE DUKERIES
SHORT CIRCULAR WALKS IN SOUTH YORKSHIRE
SHORT CIRCULAR WALKS AROUND DERBY
SHORT CIRCULAR WALKS AROUND BAKEWELL
SHORT CIRCULAR WALKS AROUND BUXTON
SHORT CIRCULAR WALKS AROUND NOTTINGHAMSHIRE
SHORT CIRCULAR WALKS ON THE NORTHERN MOORS
40 SHORT CIRCULAR PEAK DISTRICT WALKS
SHORT CIRCULAR WALKS IN THE HOPE VALLEY

DAY CHALLENGE WALKS -

JOHN MERRILL'S WHITE PEAK CHALLENGE WALK
JOHN MERRILL'S YORKSHIRE DALES CHALLENGE WALK
JOHN MERRILL'S NORTH YORKSHIRE MOORS CHALLENGE WALK
PEAK DISTRICT END TO END WALKS
THE LITTLE JOHN CHALLENGE WALK
JOHN MERRILL'S LAKELAND CHALLENGE WALK
JOHN MERRILL'S STAFFORDSHIRE MOORLAND CHALLENGE WALK
JOHN MERRILL'S DARK PEAK CHALLENGE WALK

MULTIPLE DAY WALKS -

THE RIVERS' WAY
PEAK DISTRICT HIGH LEVEL ROUTE
PEAK DISTRICT MARATHONS
THE LIMEY WAY
THE PEAKLAND WAY

COAST WALKS -

ISLE OF WIGHT COAST WALK
PEMBROKESHIRE COAST PATH
THE CLEVELAND WAY

HISTORICAL GUIDES -

DERBYSHIRE INNS
HALLS AND CASTLES OF THE PEAK DISTRICT & DERBYSHIRE
TOURING THE PEAK DISTRICT AND DERBYSHIRE BY CAR
DERBYSHIRE FOLKLORE
LOST INDUSTRIES OF DERBYSHIRE
PUNISHMENT IN DERBYSHIRE
CUSTOMS OF THE PEAK DISTRICT AND DERBYSHIRE
WINSTER — A VISITOR'S GUIDE
ARKWRIGHT OF CROMFORD
TALES FROM THE MINES by GEOFFREY CARR
PEAK DISTRICT PLACE NAMES by MARTIN SPRAY

JOHN'S MARATHON WALKS -

TURN RIGHT AT LAND'S END
WITH MUSTARD ON MY BACK
TURN RIGHT AT DEATH VALLEY
EMERALD COAST WALK

COLOUR GUIDES -

THE PEAK DISTRICT.................................Something to remember her by.

WALK RECORD CHART

Date Walked

PEAK FOREST CANAL ....

WALK 1—HYDE—4 miles ....

WALK 2—WOODLEY—4 miles ....

WALK 3—CHADKIRK—6 miles ....

WALK 4—MARPLE BRIDGE—6 miles ....

WALKS 5,6& 7—NEW MILLS—4 and 8 miles ....

WALK 8—WHALEY BRIDGE—2 miles ....

WALK 9—END TO END WALK—14¾ miles ....

MACCLESFIELD CANAL ....

WALK 1—POYNTON COPPICE—5 miles ....

WALK 2—BOLLINGTON—6 miles ....

WALKS 3,4,5& 6—MACCLESFIELD—4 miles ....

WALK 7—OAKGROVE—5 miles ....

WALK 8—OAKGROVE/GAWSWORTH HALL—4½ miles ....

WALK 9& 10—BOSLEY/THE CLOUD—4& 9 miles ....

WALK 11—MOW COP—6 miles ....

WALK 12—SCHOLAR GREEN—10 miles ....

WALK 13—HALL GREEN—5 miles ....

WALK 14—END TO END WALK—27¾ miles ....

TRENT AND MERSEY CANAL ....

WALK 1—KIDSGROVE—5 miles ....

CALDON CANAL ....

WALK 1—ALTON—5 miles ....

WALK 2& 3—FROGHALL—5& 6 miles ....

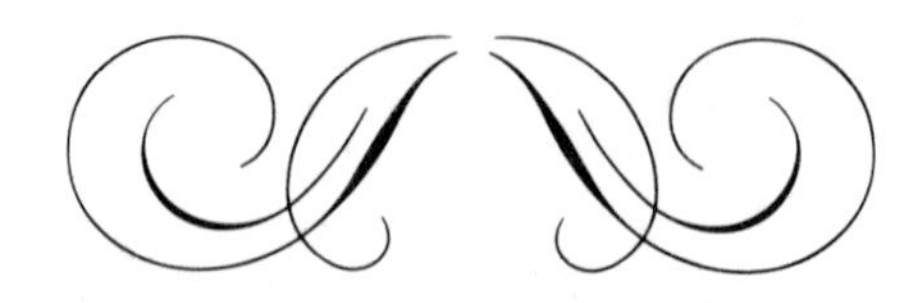

JOHN MERRILL'S CANAL WALK BADGE

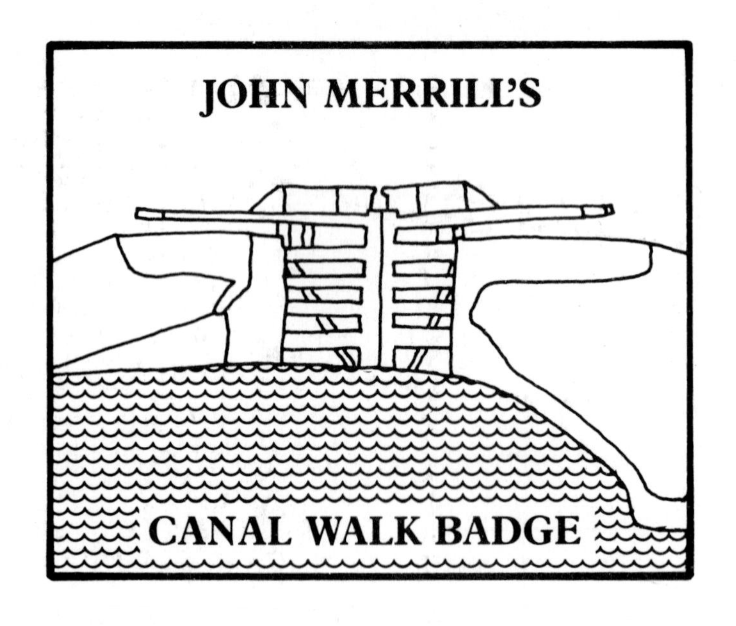

JOHN MERRILL'S CANAL WALK BADGE

Walk six or more of the walks in this book and send details to John N. Merrill at JNM PUBLICATIONS, enclosing £2.00 for a special four colour embroidered badge.